HELPING YOURSELF
TO HEALTH
FROM THE SEA

Also by the Author:

Pain-Free Living: How to Prevent and Eliminate Pain All Over the Body.

HELPING YOURSELF TO HEALTH FROM THE SEA

Howard H. Hirschhorn

Parker Publishing Company, Inc.
West Nyack, New York

This book is a reference work based on research by the author.
The opinions expressed herein are not necessarily those of or
endorsed by the publisher. The directions stated in this book are
in no way to be considered as a substitute for consultation with a
duly licensed doctor.

Library of Congress Cataloging in Publication Data

Hirschhorn, Howard H
    Helping yourself to health from the sea.

    Includes index.
    1. Sea food--Therapeutic use. 2. Therapeutics--
Popular works. 3. Thalassotherapy. I. Title.
RM231.H57   613.2'6   78-11694
ISBN 0-13-386334-4

Printed in the United States of America.

From the Seas to My Reader
and also
To the Seas

"...where great whales go sailing by,
Sail and sail with unshut eye
Around the world forever and aye."

(Matthew Arnold's *The Forsaken Merman*)

Foreword by a Marine Biologist

For twenty years I have wished for a book such as this. How many phone calls have sent me on tedious library searches about cholesterol levels in fish or recipes for the preparation of seaweeds? Or how many times has my wife searched in vain for a recipe for some unusual sea creature my students and I captured during a field trip. As a professional marine biologist, I have found Howard Hirschhorn's new book both extremely informative and entertaining. The sea food recipes alone form a monumental collection, but there is so much more for the reader.

Beginning with sea water itself, the author presents fascinating nutritional details and advice for those of us who want to intelligently use the wonderful proteins, fats and carbohydrates the sea can provide. Specific vitamins and minerals can be obtained from the sea, in their natural and unadulterated state, by selecting the proper fish or even sipping sea water. Items that many would turn up their noses at or consider "left-overs" or "trimmings" can be used for relieving indigestion, flavoring soup, or any one of a dozen other useful and health-promoting purposes. If you are healthy you can use the book to stay that way. If you are sick you may find that a faster recovery can come from the sea. If you want nice fresh fish on your table, consult this book and learn how to avoid some of the terrible stuff our supermarkets try to pass off as fish. Do you want to make your own tangy fermented fish sauces? How about keeping your skin free of wrinkles, or what about artificial seawater for baths? It's all here, even addresses of famous seaside health resorts, information on various mineral waters, suggestions for bedridden patients, a veritable ocean of information.

The nicest part of this book is that it is like visiting the man who wrote it. His conversations (just as his writings) are rich with fascinating, often humorous, personal experience gleaned from a lifetime of study and research. The reader will soon find himself in the company of a remarkable man. A world traveler, he speaks with fisherfolk in several languages as he travels along the coasts of Holland, France, Belgium, Germany and the U.S. with as much ease as you and I might go to the local grocery. In one breath he is apt to tell you how to cure a cold, discuss the differences in taste between six kinds of pickled herring, and recount a hilarious confrontation with a Dutch fisherman who refused to believe he was American. Always, he talks of the sea — where life began.

Lowell P. Thomas, Ph.D.
Professor of Biological Oceanography
University of Miami

A Word from the Author

The Sea doth wash away all human ills...

Euripides
(Greek poet, 480-406 B.C.)

All of us are still naturally attuned to the seas. Our blood is strikingly similar to the seawater that covers about three-quarters of our globe, and we can therefore claim a blood relationship with the seas. You can tap the vital forces within the oceans to reinforce your health and relieve many of the ills that plague your life.

This book tells you how to use seawater and the seacoast climate, and how to unlock the stored-up powers in the sea's plants and animals, no matter where you may live.

Turning for help to the products of the sea can yield vital health benefits. These benefits will include: (1) improved total health and resistance to disease and stress, (2) foods that provide low-cost and non-fattening nutrients, (3) increased vigor and strength, and (4) prevention or easing of many distressing conditions, such as high blood pressure, blood clots, sore throats, sexual fatigue, obesity, acid stomach and indigestion, constipation, rheumatism, urinary stones, hemorrhoids, diabetic crises, and neuralgia.

In short, you can prevent, relieve, or cure many painful or uncomfortable conditions, with the seas, the waters that come from them, and the plants and animals in them. The seas are absolutely necessary for our lives on this earth, and provide us, in addition, with a wonder-filled source for enjoying life in the best of health.

Howard H. Hirschhorn

Table of Contents

Foreword 7

A Word from the Author 9

Chapter 1   SEA FOODS, OCEANIC MOVEMENT AND
            SALT FOR HEALTHY LIVING 19

Thirteen advantages of the sea and its products   20
How seawater baths and drinks build and sustain health   22
How a seawater drink protects you from extremes   22
Fifteen uses of ordinary salt to make you feel better   23
Varieties of sea products that are good for food and health   24
How to avoid confusion in names of sea animals and plants   25

Chapter 2   HOW TO SELECT SEA NUTRIENTS FOR ENERGY,
            RESISTANCE TO INFECTION AND BODY REPAIR 27

Why proteins are so important   28
Essential amino acids from sea foods   28
Long-keeping, concentrated proteins and amino acids from
      sea foods   29
How to select sea foods for protein power and
      digestibility   30
Seaweed protein   32
Fermented fish sauce for protein-rich condiment   32
Energy-rich fats and oils in seafoods   33
Where to find healthful amounts of cholesterol in
      sea foods   35
A fish that lowers cholesterol in our blood   36

Where to find healthy carbohydrates in sea foods   36
Two particularly good sea foods for diabetics   36
Vitamins and minerals from sea foods   37
How to conserve water-soluble vitamins when cooking sea
   food   38
The sunshine vitamin = the fish vitamin   38
How a fishing boat captain selected vitamin fish   39
How to obtain more riboflavin from fish   43
How to prepare vitamin-A-rich fish   43
Important chemical elements in sea foods   44
How to evaluate daily nutritional needs   45
How to test for minerals in sea foods   45
How the old "leaf doctor" built strength, improved
   digestion and circulation   45
How a North Carolina forest warden stopped indigestion   46
Iodine — the anti-goiter element   47
Fluorine — the anti-cavity element   47
Sodium and salt — how to get it and how to get rid of it   47
Calcium — for teeth, bones, and blood clotting   49
Vitamin C and iodine from a waterside plant   49
What to bring home from the beach for invigorating,
   home-grown foods   51

**Chapter 3   HOW TO LOSE EXCESS WEIGHT WITH ANTI-
OBESITY SEA FOODS AND SEASHORE ACTIVITIES 53**

Five ways to eat and relax your excess weight away   53
How seaweed helped to burn up excess weight   54
How a dietician selected roe, fish, crustaceans and
   molluscs for calories   54

**Chapter 4   FORTY-SIX FISH TO EAT FOR HEALTHFUL
PROPORTIONS OF PROTEINS AND FATS 59**

A note on natural sauces for canned fish   68
How to select fat and protein fish   77

**Chapter 5   ROE AND CAVIAR FOR PROTEINS, AND ANTI-
DIABETIC, ANTI-ANEMIA, ANTI-EXHAUSTION
LECITHIN 79**

Varieties of roe and caviar that are good for improving
   recovery from illness   79
Why a dietician included roe in diets for certain patients   82

How a French cook prepares easily digested, nutrient-rich
    soft roe   83

**Chapter 6   MOLLUSCS THAT BRING YOU ANTI-INFECTIVE,
ANTI-TUMOR NUTRIENTS** 85

Eight molluscs that can help you fight infections   95

**Chapter 7   CRUSTACEANS THAT SUPPLY ESSENTIAL
MINERALS AND NON-FATTENING CALORIES** 97

How to steam-cook shellfish for extra flavor and extra
    wholesomeness   101

**Chapter 8   HOW TO SAFELY BUY, PREPARE AND SERVE
SEA FOODS IN ORDER TO OBTAIN THE BENEFITS OF
THEIR CURATIVE AND PREVENTIVE POWERS** 103

Seven signs of fresh, safe fish   103
How a U.S.A.F. survival expert prepared freshly caught
    aquatic food for safe eating   105
Nineteen ways of curing and preserving fish   105
Twenty-nine ways of preparing and serving fish products   108
Five enzyme-rich fermented fish sauces for activating
    cellular metabolism   113
How to pickle your own sea foods   114
How to can your own health-packed fish   118
Notes on the spices used in pickling and canning   119
Availability of turtle products that provide protein,
    energy-rich fats and miraculous curing powers   121

**Chapter 9   SEAWEEDS AND OTHER ALGAE FOR MINERALS,
VITAMINS AND RENEWED VIGOR** 123

The unique food value of seaweeds and other algae   123
How seaman E. skimmed up a balanced diet with
    silk stockings   124
Selection of seaweed for safe eating   125
Safe, palatable preparation of seaweed foods   125
Freshwater algae as healthy food   125
A vitamin-rich green seaweed salad to relieve
    discomfort   126
Brown seaweed: sea sugar and sea starch for a new twist   126
Red seaweed: a sea-rich vegetable food   128

**Chapter 10   OCEANIC MEDICINE CHEST OF CURATIVES
AND PREVENTIVES** **131**

How penguins illustrate that food heals   131
How to reduce stomach acidity with sea products   131
What Christopher Columbus and the Pasteur Institute in
    Paris learned about turtle oil   134
How Louisiana Cajuns alleviated discomfort with
    alligator tongue oil   134
How a fifty-five-year-old lady pharmacist kept her skin
    wrinkle-free   135
Effective substitutes for cod liver oil   135
How a railroader removed spots from his eyeballs   136
Six kinds of fish a Norwegian fisherman used to relieve
    his constipation   136
How an Italian fisherman alleviated abdominal
    complaints with flower-like sea anemones   136
How a Florida schoolteacher relied on sea urchins for
    health   137
A food heals and protects only if you need it   138
How a sponge diver benefited from the anti-infective
    powers of sponge   138
How a Mediterranean fisherman used starfish for
    first-aid   139
How an aged Chilean pharmacist used a whale product to
    alleviate aches   139
How sea snakes alleviated rheumatism   140
How a rural Scandinavian nurse relied on seaweed for
    all-purpose remedies   141
How a ship's physician used seaweed to alleviate his
    urinary problems   143

**Chapter 11   ENHANCING SEA FOODS WITH THE CURATIVE
AND PREVENTIVE POWERS OF LEMON, GARLIC,
ONION AND OLIVE OIL** **145**

Ten ways that lemon alleviates pain and discomfort   145
How a housewife used lemon for skin care   147
How a restauranteur overcame many kinds of gastro-
    intestinal distress   147
A seafood cocktail that lends resistance against infection,
    promotes digestion and stimulates glandular and
    kidney function   148

A seafood appetizer that fights aging and blood clots   149
Daily garlic for twenty-two reasons   149
How to prepare a winter's supply of garlic syrup to fight
     coughs   150
How a gardener used garlic for skin care   151
Twelve ways that onion fights aches and diseases, and
     regulates unbalanced body functions   151
The disinfectant powers of raw onion   152
How onions alleviate coughs and throat irritations   152
Olives — famous for thousands of years of health   154

**Chapter 12   HEALING AND REJUVENATION POWERS OF SEA,
     SAND AND SUN** **157**

How seacoast climate sustains health and alleviates
     disease   157
How seawater and mineral waters sustain health and
     alleviate disease   164
How sand and sea muds sustain health and alleviate
     disease   168
How to avoid the discomfort of skin irritations at the beach
     and in the water bikini dermatitis   169
How to protect skin from excess sun, moisture and
     dryness   172
Two methods of safely and gradually benefiting from the
     sun's healing powers   173
Advantages of seaside vacations at marinotherapeutic
     spas and resorts   175
Eighteen marinotherapeutic facilities on the
     North Sea   176
Ten marinotherapeutic spas and resorts on the
     Baltic Sea   177
A thermal institute on the Belgian coast   177
Fifteen thalassotherapeutic facilities on the Atlantic
     Ocean and the Mediterranean Sea   177
Two Spanish thalassotherapeutic and heliotherapeutic
     centers   179
Radioactive sea mud and salt water on the Adriatic Sea   180

**Chapter 13   HOW TO ENJOY THE BENEFITS OF SEAWATER
     AND OTHER CURATIVE BATHS AT HOME** **181**

How to collect and condition natural seawater   181

How to use marine salts for baths   182
Bath additives to make synthetic seawater at home   182
The advantage of hot and cold baths   183
Why Japanese women have less breast cancer   184
How wet grass increases tone and vitality   184
How to bathe to increase tone, resistance to disease,
        kidney function, and to fight obesity, insomnia,
        colds, rheumatism, lumbago, cramps, stones, and
        hemorrhoidal pain   185
How to improve circulation for bedridden persons   185
How to apply thermal packs for relieving pain, chest
        infections, phlebitis, gastrointestinal and heart
        conditions, insomnia, headache and high blood
        pressure   186
How to promote healing and lessen pain with
        compresses   186
How to wash eyes to relieve inflammation   187
How to spray water to relieve headache, insomnia, and
        rheumatism   187
How to bathe to relieve hemorrhoids, regulate
        menstruation, and alleviate the pain of stones   187
How to bathe for head-to-toe relief   188
How to normalize irregular heart action   188
How hot water soothes an irritated stomach   188
How to ease lumbago and sciatic pains   188
Herbal bath additives for added curative and
        preventive effects   189

**Chapter 14   PREPARATION OF TEAS, INFUSIONS AND
        DECOCTIONS FOR HEALING BATHS** 195

When to collect curative plants   195
How to preserve the curative ingredients of plants   196
How to prepare fresh juice to use in teas and baths   196
How to make teas, infusions and decoctions as bath
        additives   197
Why you should not mistrust all remedies that seem to
        cure too much   198

**Chapter 15   FAR EASTERN SEA PRODUCTS AVAILABLE IN
        THE U.S.A.** 199

A final look at the sea   205

HELPING YOURSELF
TO HEALTH
FROM THE SEA

1

Sea Foods, Oceanic Movement and Salt for Healthy Living

The seas and other bodies of water on our globe are the source of all earthly life, including us. And we, even this long after our beginnings in the seas millions of years ago, still continuously depend upon water. Too much of it or too little of it destroys us. On the other hand, the beneficial effects of the seas and of water *in* and *on us* assure us of the best in health and enjoyment of long life.

Each of us, before we were born, went through a stage of development that surely proved our relationship with the seas that once existed on this planet. Each and every one of us passed some time submerged in a protective sac of fluid, and we even had the vestiges of gills before we were born into this world of air.

Although it is true in principle to say that we literally carry the ocean in our bloodstream, some changes have occurred between our blood as it is now and the primeval seas in which our blood composition was probably first evolved. The similarities, however, are surprisingly greater than the differences. Seawater contains about thirty or thirty-one percent sodium, and human blood serum contains about thirty-five percent of it. Here are five other comparisons that show the similarity between seawater and blood:

	Seawater	Human blood serum
Potassium	1.1%	2.3%
Calcium	1.2%	1.2%
Chlorine	55.2%	41.3%
Magnesium	3.7%	0.3%
Sulfate	7.7%	0.2%

What does this similarity mean to us today? It means, for one thing, that we may nurture our health and satisfy some of our deep biological cravings by reaching into the seas and making use of the curative and regenerative powers inherent in water and the substances in it. There is no doubt that the oceans can provide our vital, inborn health needs.

From prehistoric times, people have been discovering new health and vitality in the sea and its products. For centuries, difficulties in keeping such products fresh, or in transporting them quickly, limited their benefits to those who lived near oceans. Now, however, modern methods of preservation, refrigeration, and transportation make it possible for all of us, no matter where we live, to take advantage of products from the sea.

Today you can find hundreds of varieties of fish and shellfish far inland, in specialty foodstores and even in many supermarkets. Food supplements derived from fish, seaweed, and seasalt may be found in most health food stores. People everywhere are learning (really re-learning) new ways of preparing dishes from the sea that are as nutritious as they are enjoyable.

THIRTEEN ADVANTAGES
OF THE SEA AND ITS PRODUCTS

Some years ago Dr. G., a nutritional chemist, fled from the turmoil of Paris and returned to his native Portugal, to a seaside town on the Atlantic coast. Here he recaptured his lost health. Despite world-renowned Parisian meals — a cuisine which included a daily serving of buttered snails — Dr. G. found his city diet was incapable of offsetting the stress of metropolitan life. He felt run-down, weak, and depressed. A year after settling in the town, breathing its salt air, eating its foods, and working as an ordinary tourist guide, Dr. G. was a new man — lively, healthy, and again enjoying life. He attributed his new-found vigor to these advantages of seafood and seaside living:

1. Fish provides easily digestible, high-value protein in abundance.
2. Most fish contains more energy-rich and nutritious muscle meat than the same amounts of land meat. Fish muscle, except muscle from sharks, rays, and similar fish, contains only about three percent of connective tissue; all the rest is meat. Land meat contains about fifteen percent of connective tissue.
3. Fish is also an excellent source of amino acids — the building blocks of which the proteins in our bodies are made.
4. Many fats in fish contain unsaturated fatty acids, which give us ready energy and may prevent atherosclerosis that could be due to blood cholesterol.
5. Roe and caviar — fish eggs — are highly nutritious, as well as helpful in sparking healthy appetites.
6. The inner organs of fish, especially the liver, are the richest known sources of vitamin A and vitamin D. Clams and other sea invertebrates (animals without backbones) are good source of vitamin B_{12}.
7. Ocean fish are a rich natural source of fluorine, and provide greater amounts of iodine than equal amounts of lean beef.
8. Fish bones (such as the easily chewable ones in canned salmon) generously supply calcium, phosphorus and iron.
9. Even cowboys and others with a he-man taste for red-blooded steak can obtain it from the sea in the form of "sea beef," or whale, and other marine mammals.
10. Seaweeds provide tasty meals loaded with valuable minerals and vitamins, a marine starch and a marine sugar (both of which may be beneficial in replacing the usual starches and sugars for some people).
11. The pulsating ocean, its currents and tides, the air near it, and its onshore and offshore breezes infuse us with the vitality of all the life in the sea and help us to get into phase with natural rhythms.
12. Seawater is a mineral-rich drink and bath that permeates the whole body.
13. Salt heals.

HOW SEAWATER BATHS AND DRINKS BUILD AND SUSTAIN HEALTH

Seawater tastes salty, but the salts dissolved in it are not all sodium chloride salt. The saltwater of the sea contains, in addition to sodium and chlorine (which make up the sodium chloride), magnesium, calcium, potassium, sulfates, strontium, bromine, boron, carbon, hydrogen, oxygen, and about another three dozen chemical elements and minerals in tiny amounts.

Bathing and swimming in the ocean expose us to all of these minerals, as well as to the enzymes, vitamins, amino acids, and antibiotics dissolved in it, to the stimulating yet calming waves and currents, and to the actual living quality provided by vast quantities of visible and microscopic life in the water. Extensive research into the creation of artificial seawater has failed to show us how to completely reproduce actual seawater precisely, because of this vital living quality. However, there are several ways to prepare usable synthetic seawater. Details of how to make effective use of seawater, as well as how to make synthetic seawater, are given elsewhere in this book.

Can you drink seawater? Yes and no. No, if you're on a liferaft and you guzzle down saltwater because you are suffering from thirst. Yes, if you are drinking only a little bit and not taking in more salt than you would otherwise do by using salt on your food. Melanesians drink seawater with their meals. Pacific islanders on Tahiti, Samoa and the Tongas dip their raw food into bowls of seawater, or simply into the sea itself if they are eating close to it. At spas where seawater is featured as a health drink, it is sometimes flavored in various ways to make it more palatable. A suitable diet, too, goes along with the drinking of seawater in order to help you handle the excess sodium you take in during these courses of treatment.

HOW A SEAWATER DRINK PROTECTS YOU FROM EXTREMES

Frederick S. was somewhat surprised when physicians at a German North Sea resort suggested that he drink a cup of seawater every few hours to *reduce* his stomach acidity, yet also suggested the same thing to another patient to *increase* his stomach acidity! The secret is that seawater is a *normalizer* of body functions.

FIFTEEN USES OF ORDINARY SALT
TO MAKE YOU FEEL BETTER

At an international medical meeting in Miami Beach where new treatments with modern drugs were being discussed, I overheard a snowy-haired physician say, "Pooh, who needs a cannon when a slingshot will do nicely?" The moment I asked that physician about his slingshot cures, he took me by the arm and led me out of the huge, darkened lecture hall, through the hotel lobby and out on the beach, where he took half a dozen deep breaths of the fresh sea breeze, did half a dozen side-straddle hops, and then confided in me about his use of salt. Here are fifteen ways he used it to alleviate the ills of his patients over the years:

1. *Head cold* — Mix one teaspoon of salt in a cup of milk and two glasses of warm water. Use a small, infant-sized rubber syringe to squirt the mixture into your nasal passages; the liquid will run back through your nose into your throat from where you can spit it out. Or you can hold some of the mixture in your cupped hand and draw it into your nostrils. Until you get used to it, it may feel like you are drowning, but you are not. Relief is immediate.

2. *Toothache* — Mix a pinch of salt with a pinch of alum, daub a piece of moist cotton in the mixture and pack it into your cavity (if that is the cause of the ache). After a feeling of coldness in the tooth, pain gradually subsides.

3. *Sore throat* — Gargling with a few teaspoons of salt in a glass of warm water affords almost instant relief. It also acts as a mild antiseptic and helps control any possible infection.

4. *Indigestion and heartburn* — Let a small pinch of salt dissolve in your mouth for prompt relief.

5. *Indigestion and stomachache* — A teaspoon of dry salt may help, although you may need a sip of water to get it down.

6. *Diarrhea* — A small pinch of salt in a tablespoon of fresh lemon juice may help. In some cases you may find it better to repeat this every two hours until the diarrhea stops.

7. *Vomiting of blood* — A teaspoon of dry salt may help control the hemorrhage until medical help is obtained.

8. *Irritated eyes* — A small pinch of salt in two tablespoons of cooled, boiled water makes a soothing eyewash for many conditions that cause irritation.

9. *Chronic joint pain* — A very concentrated solution of salt, rubbed well into the skin over the joint, may ease pain.

10. *Festered finger and nailbed* — Prepare a poultice of a teaspoon of salt (roasted dry over the range or in the oven); a teaspoon of good quality, non-perfumed soap (scrape it off the bar of soap); and a teaspoon of turpentine (preferably from the larch tree). Apply twice a day. The festered part should open within four days or so and let the pus escape. When this happens, wash well with soap and water, apply an antiseptic and bandage.

11. *Sprains and bruises* — Add good brandy to half a bottle of dry salt until almost filled. Shake and let the contents settle before soaking a compress or cloth with it and applying it to the affected part. This should not only alleviate immediate pain, but also speed healing.

12. *Itching hives* — A warm saltwater bath (two ounces of salt to thirty gallons of warm water) quickly alleviates itching.

13. *Fainting spells, fits and convulsions* — A pinch of dry salt on the tongue often helps to calm down the victim.

14. *Headaches associated with menopause* — Mix four tablespoons of spirits of ammonia (not kitchen ammonia!), a tablespoon of salt, six tablespoons of bay rum and a quart of water. Soak a compress in the mixture and apply it to the forehead of the reclining victim. Relief is fast — probably as fast as the victim can take several deep, relaxing breaths.

15. *General tonic* — Small amounts of salt stimulate (larger amounts act either as a laxative or an emetic), aid digestion, tone up the body in general and are mildly antiseptic. Although not at all a substitute for actual ocean bathing, a useful salt bath can be prepared by dissolving a pound of salt in four gallons of water. A shower removes the excess salt (that is, the salt that your body has not absorbed during the bath). Ways of preparing artificial seawater are given elsewhere in this book.

VARIETIES OF SEA PRODUCTS
THAT ARE GOOD FOR FOOD AND HEALTH

Here is a simple classification system as an aid to remembering all the different kinds of sea life you will encounter in this book and in the markets now that you are making yourself particularly aware of health from the sea.

The *vertebrates* (animals with backbones) include:

1. Marine mammals (whales, seals, etc.)
2. Marine reptiles (sea snakes, turtles, etc.)
3. Fish (most fish on the market are the bony kind as opposed to the kind with cartilage instead of bone, such as sharks and rays)

Then there are the *invertebrates* (animals without backbones):

1. Crustaceans (lobsters, crabs, crayfish, crawfish, shrimps, prawns, barnacles)
2. Molluscs (oysters, clams, scallops, abalone, snails, octopus, squid)
3. Innumerable other kinds (starfish, sea urchins, anemones, jellyfish, sea cucumbers, etc.)

And finally there is the *plant world,* consisting of seaweed or marine algae, freshwater algae, and waterside plants. (Major R., a U.S. Army paratrooper, by way of illustrating the advantages of waterside plants, relieved the stings of bees, wasps and hornets by rubbing the stung spots with juice squeezed from the crushed leaves of the climbing hemp weed, which grows near the seaside, along streams and in marshy ground.)

HOW TO AVOID CONFUSION
IN NAMES OF SEA ANIMALS AND PLANTS

You may note that when you shop for fish and other sea foods, the names under which they are sold may be confusing. *Rock salmon* can mean dogfish, coalfish, marine catfish, etc. Lake herring (alias chub, cisco, tullibee, lakefish) is a freshwater fish; real herrings live in seawater. Autumn albacore is yellowfin tuna. Spiny lobster is crawfish. American butterfish (alias dollar fish, sheephead, pumpkin scad) is also called a starfish (the same as the five-armed invertebrate that looks like a star).

The use of internationally known names in Latin helps to avoid confusion. Because local names for animals and plants vary so much, the internationally used scientific name in Latin helps you to overcome local language differences and positively identify the plant or animal you want. Two fish might have the same common name in one place, but their different scientific names readily identify them as two different kinds, such as, for example, a coalfish. One fish called "coalfish" is really *Anopoploma fimbria* from the Pacific

Ocean, and the other "coalfish" is *Pollachius virens* from the Atlantic Ocean. Luckily, however, the Pacific coalfish can also be called a sablefish, and the Atlantic coalfish can also be called saithe!

Or, one fish may be called by several different names, but it will have only one scientific name. This means you are probably dealing only with nicknames for a single kind of fish, such as, for example, common sole, black sole, Dover sole, Parkgate sole, river sole, sea partridge, slip, Southport sole, true sole, and tongue — all the same fish called *Solea solea* by its international scientific name.

Happy and healthful eating!

2
How to Select Sea Nutrients
for Energy, Resistance to Infection
and Body Repair

The cells of your body require nourishment. For your good health, your cells must have proteins, lipids (fats and oils), carbohydrates, minerals, vitamins, and even water. These are all essential ingredients for your energy and growth, the repair of your tissues, and synthesis of vital substances such as enzymes within your body.

Even non-nutrients in foods play vital roles in your system. For example, cellulose, the substance that makes up the cell walls of plants (and that makes celery crunchy), is one of these important non-nutrients. Human beings can't digest cellulose, but they need it for roughage, or bulk, to help move food smoothly along the digestive tract.

When you eat a broad and varied diet, you help make certain that you get what your body cells need — including not only the nutrients, but also the seldom-recognized "extras" in foods that may also be vital to your health. Foods from the sea are important sources of both nutrients and non-nutrients.

Seafoods are particularly good sources of proteins, so let's talk about proteins first.

WHY PROTEINS ARE SO IMPORTANT

Protein builds and repairs all of your body tissues, forms antibodies within you to combat infection, and provides you with energy for everyday living. Hemoglobin, the oxygen-carrying red pigment in your blood, is a protein. Enzymes, the key substances that let your body "burn the fuel" you eat — that is, transform your food into energy for your life processes and into body-building blocks, are also proteins.

Your digestive processes break down the proteins you eat into basic building blocks called *amino acids.* You absorb amino acids into your cells, where they are built up again into proteins, but this time as proteins that are *you.* That is, the amino acids are jumbled about and repatterned so that they now build *you* (or build *me* when *I* eat them) instead of coming together again as the original food.

A deficiency in *essential* amino acids (that is, a lack of those amino acids that you *have to* take in with your food because your body can't manufacture them) can stunt your growth, hamper repair and replacement of your tissues, degenerate your muscles, deplete your energy, and cause a loss of your vitality and vigor. You can supply yourself with these essentials most enjoyably by eating plenty of sea foods, which are generally an excellent source of healthy amino acids.

ESSENTIAL AMINO ACIDS FROM SEA FOODS

The comparison below of the percentage of essential amino acids in the protein portion of three ounces (about a hundred grams) of fish and beef shows that fish contains about as much of these essential building blocks as beef:

Essential amino acid	% amino acid in protein part of 3 ounces (100 grams) of fish	% amino acid in protein part of 3 ounces (100 grams) of beef
Lysine	9%	8%
Leucine	7%	7%
Valine	5.8%	5.8%
Phenylalamine	4.5%	4.9%
Isoleucine	6%	6.3%
Threonine	4.5%	4.6%
Methionine	3.5%	3.3%
Histidine	2.4%	2.9%
Tryptophan	1.3%	1.9%
Arginine	7.4%	7.7%

Scientific studies made with different kinds of fish showed that a 150-pound man who ate six ounces of fish fillet consumed *more* of the following amino acids than his daily nutritional needs called for:

- Lysine — twice the amount (or 200%) of his daily need
- Threonine — over a half more (or 160%) of his daily need
- Isoleucine — almost a half more (or 140%) of his daily need
- Leucine — a quarter more (or 125%) of his daily need
- Valine — a quarter more (or 125%) of his daily need

LONG-KEEPING, CONCENTRATED PROTEINS AND AMINO ACIDS FROM SEA FOODS

While you may never eat bread or flour made of fish meal, you may be interested to learn how much nutrition there is in such meal. In other countries, people have traditionally made and eaten a form of meal made of fish. Now, modern technology has enabled the United States and other industrialized countries to produce edible, nutritious fish meal concentrates to feed a hungry world. Tests of fish meal or flour conducted in the United States, and in Malaya, India, Chile, and other nations showed that this substance is a valuable source of protein, concentrated in form and relatively easy to store for long periods.

Tests of fish biscuits, shark-flour bread, and protein supplements for children, fish-flour formulas for babies, and general use of fish flour as a meat substitute show:

Malayan children do well on fish biscuits: Several hundred children and their mothers in the Federation of Malaya who ate biscuits made from defatted sardine meal or flour gained significantly more weight than did others who were given skimmed milk but no biscuits made from sardine flour. The fish biscuits contained about two-thirds more of the amino acid lysine than did the skimmed milk. (Gaining weight, of course, is not necessarily a sign of health for an adult; but it is a good sign in undernourished or convalescing adults, or in growing children.)

Shark flour bread: The ocean is a limitless storehouse of usable protein, and has been estimated to grow enough sea food every year to keep ten times today's human population of the world healthy. Research is constantly focussing on what can be eaten or otherwise utilized to our advantage. In India, investigators developed a process to produce urea-free shark flour with 90% protein. (Sharks are roving, carrion-feeding scavengers that build up a distastefully large amount of urea and an ammoniacal stench in their flesh because of their meat diet. So, a urea-free product would make some sharks more palatable.) Bread baked from 5% shark flour and the rest as wheat flour was tasted and approved by a whole panel of tasters. As a matter of fact, wheat enriched with fish protein concentrate and formulated for local tastes at many places in the world has already been made into acceptably nutritious foods.

Fish protein supplement for children: In the U.S.A., the Federal Food, Drug and Cosmetic Act permits twenty grams a day of fish protein concentrate (made from whole, wholesome hake and hake-like fish without removal of heads, fins, tails, or entrails) for use as a protein supplement in food for children under eight years of age.

Baby's formula made with fish flour: A factory in Chile sponsored by UNICEF (United Nations International Childrens Emergency Fund) produced a defatted, deodorized flour from hake for use in a baby formula. This formula was bottle-fed to nine normal babies ranging in age from three to six months, and was found to be quite adequate as a source of protein for them.

Fish flour equals beef and eggs in children's diet: Pediatricians, trying to solve nutritional problems in certain tropical areas, supplemented a rice diet with fish flour for feeding convalescent children. A diet of milk + beef + fish + eggs + bread + mixed vegetables was compared with an experimental diet of fish flour + mixed vegetables. The fish flour was first cooked in coconut milk with curry powder and salt. About twenty grams were served with lunch and dinner, along with rice bread and vegetables. Results: height, weight, proteins in the blood and amount of oxygen-carrying hemoglobin in the blood's red blood cells all increased in both diet groups. This meant that the fish protein flour was able to replace beef and eggs in the diet of these children.

HOW TO SELECT SEA FOODS
FOR PROTEIN POWER AND DIGESTIBILITY

Deborah D. decided to select sea foods for proteins because her family was on the heavy side and wanted to eat more fish and less land meat. Her research through the nutrition books showed that there are about seventeen to nineteen grams of protein in a hundred grams (about three ounces) of dried herring, sprat or brisling, haddock and cod. There are fifteen to twenty grams in a hundred grams of dried eel, and nineteen to twenty-one grams in a hundred grams of dried salmon. By comparison, a hundred grams of lean pork or beef contains twenty grams of protein. The protein content of fish muscle generally increases as you go towards the tail. Fats, on the other hand, tend to increase as you go toward the head. Light meat tends to contain more protein and less fat; dark meat, by contrast, tends to contain less protein, but much more fat.

Claus R., a research chemist in a leading sea food cannery, extensively investigated food elements in various forms of sea food. He found these percentages of protein in each one-hundred grams of various canned sea foods:

100 grams of canned sea food	% protein
Dry-pack shrimp	27%
Tuna	27%
Salmon	21%
Sardines in oil	21%
Mackerel	21%
Sardines in tomato sauce	18%
Regular-pack shrimp	15%

He also found the following percentages of protein in each one-hundred grams of various fish flours or meals:

100 grams of flour or meal from	% protein
Steam-dried cod	63.9%
Fat herring	61.3%
Salt herring	56.2%
Herring scraps	55.4%
Air-dried cod	54.2%
Cod liver	49.5%
Fresh herring	16%
Fresh cod	14.6%
Cod heads and entrails	13.8%

From the above, we can easily see that flour or meal made from sea foods can be a concentrated source of protein. Claus, the chemist, reported that the most digestible of these fish meal proteins are those from salt herring (98% digestibility), and from steam-dried or air-dried cod (94% digestibility).

SEAWEED PROTEIN

Seaweed (marine alga) farming is a serious affair in some countries, and quite promising as a source of protein in parts of the world where animal proteins are scarce. Algae (plural of alga) are efficient converters of the sun's energy into food — twenty to forty times more efficient than more traditional crops like soybeans, cereals and corn. Although alga contains less protein than meat or fish, it contains more than legumes (beans, peas, etc.), cereals and most hays. Alga also contains a surprising amount of vitamins.

FERMENTED FISH SAUCE
FOR PROTEIN-RICH CONDIMENT

While with her husband, who was stationed in the Philipine Islands, Clarissa Y. made a valuable discovery about sauces. Because of her finicky eating habits, Clarissa had long been underweight and lacking in energy. Nothing seemed to help until she learned to eat the zesty, enzyme-rich, fermented fish sauces of the Islands. Sauces like *patis* not only sparked her sometimes poor appetite, but also provided an exciting way to supplement her protein intake. Unlike other protein-rich foods, *patis* did not make her feel stuffed or bloated. Her weight gain was noticeable within a few weeks, and she almost immediately began to feel more alert and energetic.

To make *patis,* Clarissa first had to prepare *bagoong* — which is a fine appetizer or snack any time of the day. Philippine *bagoong* and *patis* can be made from fish or shrimp, and even from the roe of these animals. The dish is in the form of a mash, which may take as long as a year to ferment, or age, after the whole fish, or pounded fish or shrimp, is packed with salt (20% to 25% by weight). For milder aroma, it should be aged a shorter time.

Clarissa prepared her mash according to these recommendations (based upon research supported by the U.S. Department of the Interior):

1. Use only good, fresh fish, preferably anchovies.
2. Wash the fish in clean, fresh water.
3. Mix the fish with clean, pure salt (two to seven parts of salt by weight).
4. Protect the mix from insects, and excessive exposure to air, by storing it in a warm place with very little circulating air.

5. When the developing aroma suits your taste (after at least several weeks) drain off the free liquid (that's your fish sauce or *patis)*.
6. Grind up the semi-solid remainder (that's your *bagoong)*.
7. Strain the *patis* and store it in clean bottles with small necks, such as wine or catsup bottles.
8. Pack the *bagoong* into clear containers and use it as snack food. Refrigeration tends to retard the further development of the aroma, so if it is just strong enough for your taste, cool it as it is.
9. The *bagoong* aging or ripening process in Step 4, can be speeded up by maintaining a temperature of 113°F for a week or two at some time during the whole ripening period.
10. Air-tight containers are the first choice for keeping *bagoong* as it ages; otherwise, large deep containers are the next best choice.
11. Use of pure salt causes a more rapid liquefaction and disintegration of the solids, a greater percentage of proteins in the liquid layer (the sauce or *patis),* and less problems with bacteria doing other than what they are supposed to do — to make good *bagoong* and *patis.*

Other fermented fish foods are discussed in Chapter 8. Fermented sauces made from fish and other natural substances are available in ready-made form from Japanese and Chinese food distributors in the United States.

ENERGY-RICH FATS AND OILS IN SEA FOODS

Fats and oils, or lipids, are twice as energy-rich as either proteins or carbohydrates. Your sea meals can pack a lot of power in small portions. Fish lipids may be concentrated in the livers of fish, such as in cod, or distributed throughout the whole fish, such as in herring (particularly the belly and near the dorsal or top fin). Fish contain less fat than land meat does; this is true even for fatty fish such as salmon. Preserved fish, on the other hand, are high in fat. An ounce of canned sardines may equal a chicken egg in fat content.

Fats and oils, like other nutrients in sea foods, vary according to the kind of sea food and at what time of the year it was caught. A small, immature herring, for example, might contain 8% fat in the summer, a winter herring might contain 13% fat, and a spent (that is, spawned) herring only 3%. Eulachon, a smelt, on the other hand, is also called *candlefish* because when it is dried it is oily enough to be lit and burned as a candle!

In his studies, Claus R., the cannery chemist, found the following approximate percentages of fat in each one-hundred grams of various *fresh* fish:

100 grams of fish	% fats and oils
Cod liver	40 to 70%
Eel	15 to 30%
Herring	5 to 20%
Sprat or brisling	5 to 15%
Salmon	2 to 15%
Haddock	0 to 1%
Cod	0 to 1% (If this seems low for cod, it is because all the fats and oils of this fish are in its liver.)

Claus found the following percentages of fats and oils in each one-hundred grams of various *canned* sea foods:

100 grams of sea food	% fats and oils
Sardines	20%
Tuna	20%
Mackerel	12%
Salmon	7%
Dry-pack shrimp	2%
Regular-pack shrimp	0.7%

And he found the following percentages of fats and oils in fish flours or meal:

100 grams of flour or meal from	% fats and oils
Cod liver	31.0%
Fresh herring	12.5%
Herring scraps	12.3%
Fat herring	11.7%
Salt herring	7.7%
Lean herring with less than 3% salt	3.8%
Steam-dried cod	2.4%
Air-dried cod	1.9%
Fresh cod	1.5%
Cod heads and entrails	1.4%

Claus believes that the most digestible of these fish meal scraps are those from herring scrap (100% digestibility), fresh cod and fresh herring (99% digestibility), and salt herring (98% digestibility).

WHERE TO FIND HEALTHFUL AMOUNTS
OF CHOLESTEROL IN SEA FOODS

Medical authorities have expressed concern that too much cholesterol in the diet of some people may be harmful. Excessive cholesterol may deposit fatty substances along the inside walls of blood vessels, and thus it may contribute to hardening of these vessels and to other signs of atherosclerosis.

Medical scientists know, however, that *all* people with large amounts of cholesterol do not necessarily have atherosclerosis or other cardiovascular diseases. They also know that *all* people with atherosclerosis or other cardiovascular diseases do not necessarily have large amounts of cholesterol in their blood. It is known, too, that cholesterol is part of your normal healthy body processes. Cholesterol in your skin, for example, is changed to vitamin D (the sunshine vitamin) by the sun's ultraviolet radiation.

In other words, a certain amount of cholesterol in your body is desirable, and sea foods can provide it in healthful amounts.

Claus analyzed one-hundred grams each of various sea foods and compared these with the same amounts of chicken, eggs, and beef. He found the following amounts of cholesterol in each one-hundred-gram portion:

100 grams of food	Cholesterol (milligrams)
Fish fillet or fish steak	70 mg
Shrimp	125 mg
Oysters	less than 200 mg.
Lobster	200 mg
Beef	70 mg
Fresh egg yolk	1500 mg!

There is no need for you to shy away from any cholesterol in sea food, for sea food also acts to protect you from hypercholesterolemia (cholesterol in the blood). Fish oils, rich in polyunsaturated fatty acids, are known to lower the amount of cholesterol in the blood. In tests, the fresh flour or meal made from various fish (menhaden, mullet, salmon, perch, etc.) quickly reduced the amount of cholesterol in the blood of rats; oil pressed from the meal had the same effect. Scientists who studied the effect of fish oils on cholesterol in the blood of people recommended that we eat fish meat from the body of the fish rather than too many fish liver oils, because fish liver can contain large amounts of concentrated vitamins A and D, and overdosages of these vitamins might not be good for us.

A FISH THAT LOWERS CHOLESTEROL IN OUR BLOOD

Studies at the University of Hamburg and elsewhere revealed that miners in vanadium mines had less cholesterol in the blood, and, amazingly, those miners had less atherosclerosis than people who worked outside of the mines. Scientists then tried giving vanadium to rats and rabbits, and thereby verified the fact that vanadium does lower cholesterol in the blood.

A good source of *trace* amounts (that is, naturally occurring, non-poisonous amounts) of vanadium is sardines. A diet of sardines has in fact not only prevented an increase in the blood cholesterol of experimental rats, but has also actually *lowered* the amount of cholesterol in "sick" hypercholesteremic rats (rats which were purposely given excessive amounts of cholesterol).

WHERE TO FIND
HEALTHY CARBOHYDRATES IN SEA FOODS

Your body cells derive energy from carbohydrates — starches and sugars. If your body does not burn them all up, and they exceed the liver's capacity to store them, then they may turn into fat. Carbohydrates from sea foods, however, are not likely to fatten you.

The seaweeds, not fish, are where the carbohydrates are in the sea. The percentage of carbohydrates in canned mackerel, salmon, sardines, shrimp and tuna, for example, are all less than 1% of the total nutrients. The little carbohydrate that is present in fresh fish is mostly concentrated as glycogen (or animal starch) in their livers.

The meat and juices of raw hard or round clams, however, can contain 4½% carbohydrate; and, if you make clam fritters (with eggs, milk and the other ingredients for a good batter), the carbohydrates can shoot up to 31%! So, it is not always *what* you eat, but *how* you eat it, that determines your carbohydrate intake.

TWO PARTICULARLY GOOD SEA FOODS FOR DIABETICS

Judy R., a nurse who specializes in caring for diabetics, let some of her patients on restricted diets eat oysters and clams for four reasons:

1. Oysters and clams taste good enough to make eating en-

joyable and not another chore (which restricted diets tend to become for diabetics).

2. Oysters and clams satisfy hunger because they are bulky; six oysters make a meal.

3. A meal of six oysters or clams on the half shell, amounting to a hundred grams of edible foodstuff, is a balanced snack, yet contains so few carbohydrates (really glycogen, which is animal carbohydrate stored in the liver), fats and proteins that they can usually be disregarded when adding up the daily allowable quantities for strictly controlled diets.

4. Copper, often higher in shellfish than in fish, is believed to extend the effect of insulin. (Zinc, often concentrated in oysters, activates insulin.)

VITAMINS AND MINERALS FROM SEA FOODS

Six ounces of a fatty fish fillet (all edible parts, no bones) provide a 150-pound man with the following:

- 1000% (or two and a half times more) of his daily vitamin D needs
- 100% (or all) of his daily vitamin A needs
- 75% of his daily niacin needs
- 60% of his daily fat needs
- 50% of his daily protein needs
- 45% of his daily phosphorus needs
- 30% of his daily iron needs
- 30% of his daily vitamin B_2 or riboflavin needs
- 25% of his daily caloric requirement
- 15% of his daily B_1 or thiamine needs

If the six ounces of fish are not from a fatty species, but from a lean one (lean fish are called *white* fish, written in two words), then the amount of vitamin B_1 is about the same. However, the other nutrients are less and there is no vitamin A and no vitamin D.

Any list of actual amounts of vitamins in so much fish weight gives you only a general idea of relative amounts. For vitamins, like other nutrients, vary according to the kind of fish (or other animal), how old it is when caught, where it is caught and during what season, how it is cured or preserved, and, finally, how it is cooked.

HOW TO CONSERVE WATER-SOLUBLE VITAMINS
WHEN COOKING SEA FOOD

How you prepare sea food may determine how much of its vitamin content is lost in the cooking water. Also, juices and packing liquids of canned foods contain significant amounts of water-soluble vitamins (B complex and vitamin C); drink this juice or include it if possible in the dish you are preparing. According to the United States Department of Agriculture, about a third of the water-soluble nutrients in canned vegetables are in the liquid, and they recommend that you use this liquid as soon as possible to avoid losses incurred by merely letting it stand in the light and air. Their recommendations for using canned vegetable liquids can also be applied to sea food:

1. Boil down the liquid and serve it mixed with the solids.
2. Heat the liquid and serve it as an appetizer.
3. Use the liquid in soups and gravies.

THE SUNSHINE VITAMIN = THE FISH VITAMIN

Vitamin D is called the *sunshine* vitamin because it is formed when ultraviolet radiation from the sun (direct and not filtered through a glass window) irradiates skin cholesterol.

Vitamin D is also called the *fish* vitamin because it is found in the liver and/or whole body of many kinds of fish. Like all good things, too much can be bad for you. Excessive amounts of vitamin D (such as might occur in an overdosage with too many vitamin pills) can cause too much calcium in the blood and tissues, resulting in stomach distress and even growth retardation in growing children. In the proper amount, which comes from a good diet, vitamin D regulates the body's use of calcium and phosphorus in bones and teeth and normalizes blood. Too little vitamin D leads to swollen ankles and wrists, abnormal bones and teeth in youngsters and softening of bone in adults.

Although the meat of some fish contains various amounts of vitamin D, you will find the greatest vitamin D content in the fat from the viscera or internal organs of freshwater fish like carp, bream, roach, lamprey, pike-perch, and marine fish like Japanese sardines, Atlantic redfish, menhaden, mackerel skipjack, Atlantic and Pacific bluefin tuna, yellowfin tuna, albacore tuna, swordfish, red cod, Atlantic and Pacific halibut, etc. Canning or storage does not appreciably reduce the amount of vitamin D.

If you eat herrings and sardines often, you probably take in quite enough vitamin D for your daily needs. A serving of herring, for example, gives you not only more than your daily need of vitamin D, but also about a half of your daily requirement for vitamin A.

HOW A FISHING BOAT CAPTAIN
SELECTED VITAMIN FISH

Eugene V., captain of a fishing boat, came to the U.S.A. from northern Europe, where he sailed with Baltic and North Sea fishing fleets for many years. He now operates an Atlantic coast fishing boat and a small fish packing firm. "My boat is for real living, and my packing firm is only for making a living," as he put it.

"Laboratory evaluations of the vitamins in fish," Captain Eugene said, "tell us a lot of useful things; but fish, even the same kind from one fishing ground, sometimes vary tremendously from season to season or even during the same fishing season. I have my own private list of vitamin-finding rules. I think my taste buds had something to do with my choices, though, because some other fish have vitamins, too, but I just don't like to eat those kinds." I compared Captain Eugene's list of vitamin fish with U. S. Department of Agriculture and United Nations nutritional statistics, and found that vitamins had indeed been identified in most of the fish on his list. Captain Eugene's years of experience provided the following rules for finding vitamin fish.

Captain Eugene's rules
for finding vitamin-A fish

1. Rapacious fish such as tuna, cod, halibut, and most sharks accumulate vitamin A. Among freshwater fish, good sources are northern pike, perch, and pike-perch.

2. Dark meat of most bony fish (but not cartilaginous ones like sharks) usually contains somewhat more vitamin A than white meat. More vitamin A is usually in the deeper tissues rather than in the parts closer to the outside walls of the fish.

3. More vitamin A is up front than in the hinder parts of the big-eyed tuna.

4. Fish eyes, especially of freshwater fish, contain vitamin A, the amount of which does not vary as much (because of changes in

season, feeding habits, age, etc.) as the vitamin A in other parts of the fish. Fish chowder that includes the head (or at least the eyes) thus makes a vitamin-A richer meal than fish soup made with fillet alone.

5. The digestive tract of Japanese lamprey is richer in vitamin A than is any other living substance we use for food. (A Japanese cook told me that the skin slime should be washed off.)

6. The liver of the following fish is rich in vitamin A: swordfish, soupfin shark, rockfish, chub mackerel, Pacific halibut, red steenbras, Atlantic yellowfish tuna.

7. The meat of the following fish is rich in vitamin A:

- Japanese lamprey (eaten by the Japanese as a remedy for night blindness)
- Swordfish
- Freshwater eel
- Dogfish
- Lanternfish
- Lizardfish
- Conger eel
- Blenny
- Harvest fish
- Alfonsino
- Hogfish
- Parrotfish
- Gray mullet
- Japanese sea bass
- Japanese salmon
- Pacific cod
- Alaska pollack
- Common grouper
- Yellowfin tuna
- Bluefin tuna
- Porgy (the skin is twice as rich in vitamin A as the meat)

Captain Eugene's seven rules
for finding vitamin-B_1 sources

1. Codfish from northern waters contains more B_1 than cod from warmer seas.

2. The livers of marine mammals (whale, seal) contain more vitamin B_1 than the livers of farm animals.

3. Fish eyes, especially of the pollack, contain more B_1 than the eyes of land animals; so include pollack eyes in your fish chowders.

4. The skin, especially from the back, of Japanese lampreys contains much more B_1 than found in other fish.

5. The dark meat of the following fish is especially high in vitamin B_1: chub mackerel, skipjack, bluefin and yellowfin tuna.

6. The livers of the following fish are particularly rich in vitamin B_1: skipjack, yellowfin tuna, horse mackerel, chub mackerel, Japanese eel, rockfish.

7. An enzyme in some freshwater fish such as carp destroys vitamin B_1. To preserve B_1 in freshly caught fish, remove the organs and gills (which harbor those B_1-destructive enzymes) as soon as possible. Clams, too, lose B_1 from this enzyme, so eat the clams soon (when still alive), or else freeze or cook them immediately. (When eating fresh, raw clams and oysters from suspected waters, be sure to first let them flush themselves clean overnight in a tank of fresh seawater. Reputable dealers and restaurants obtain their molluscs from fisherman who do this.)

Captain Eugene's two rules
for finding vitamin-C fish

1. Vitamin C is highest in the brain, liver and kidney of saltwater fish in the summer.

2. Cod roe is rich in vitamin C.

Captain Eugene's two rules
for finding vitamin-E fish

1. Cod roe contains about as much vitamin E as cereal germ.

2. Oil from the liver of the following fish contains large amounts of vitamin E: turbot, angler, cod, ling, blue rayfish, haddock.

Captain Eugene's rule
for finding vitamin-B_6 fish

Pacific sardines, mackerel, saury and herring contain significant amounts of vitamin B_6 (pyridoxine or the antidermatitis factor).

Captain Eugene's five rules
for finding vitamin-B_{12} fish

1. Dark meat contains more vitamin B_{12} (cyanocobalamine or the antipernicious anemia factor) than light meat. Dark-fleshed fish

include lamprey, sardine, herring. A tuna's dark meat is richer in B_{12} than its white meat.

2. The liver of the following fish is particularly rich in B_{12} (and may provide as much of it as does beef liver): yellowfin and bluefin tunas, Atlantic mackerel, herring.

3. The spleen of many of the above fish contains B_{12}.

4. Pollack heart is extremely rich in B_{12}.

5. Clams and oysters are rich in B_{12}.

Captain Eugene's rules
for finding niacin in fish

Japanese mackerel, skipjack, frigate mackerel, and Atlantic mackerel are good sources of niacin (the anti-pellagra vitamin), as are, in general, the fatter fishes, as well as the more active and mobile ones.

Captain Eugene's rule
for finding folic acid in fish

Eel, lamprey, mullet and goby contain large amounts of folic acid (which is involved in our blood-building system). In general, the active kinds of fish contain more folic acid than the sedentary kinds, and white meat contains more than dark meat.

Captain Eugene's three rules
for finding vitamin-B_2 fish

1. The meat of the following fish, and the livers of many of them, contain sizeable amounts of vitamin B_2:

- Japanese jack mackerel
- Lamprey
- Atlantic mackerel
- Atlantic herring
- Pacific herring
- Rainbow trout
- Chub mackerel
- Atlantic cod
- Skipjack

2. There is more B_2 in cod from northern waters than from warmer ones.

3. The back skin of lamprey is rich in B_2.

HOW TO OBTAIN MORE RIBOFLAVIN FROM FISH

For riboflavin, or vitamin B_2, Captain Eugene took care to eat the skin on the proper side of his vitamin fish. He paid attention to the report of the Food and Agricultural Organization of the United Nations that skin on the eyed side of flatfish (flounders, etc.) has up to about sixty-five times more riboflavin content than the blind side. (Adult flounders and other flatfish have both eyes on the same side of the head.) The back skin of the albacore tuna has about twice the riboflavin of the belly skin. The back skin of the mackerel has about four times the riboflavin of the belly skin.

HOW TO PREPARE VITAMIN-A-RICH FISH

A Japanese engineer, Kanji S., learned from the Food and Agricultural Organization of the United Nations that lamprey and eel contained large amounts of vitamin A in their meat, and thus differed from many other fish in which most of the vitamin A is in the liver and entrails, not the meat. Skipjack tuna entrails, for example, contain ninety-nine times more vitamin A than the fish's meat. Lamprey entrails contain about twice as much vitamin A as its meat. Eel meat, on the other hand, contains about four times more vitamin A than its entrails.

Because Kanji S.'s work as an engineer brought him into contact with rural villagers all along the coasts of his country, he used the opportunity to learn more about the traditional foods of his people, particularly the foods that were recognized as especially healthful ones. Lamprey and eel were such foods, and here is how they were prepared:

1. Slit the eel or lamprey open lengthwise.
2. Remove the entrails and the spine. (Save the eel entrails, but not those from the lamprey.)
3. Skewer on bamboo splinters and broil over glowing charcoal until ready to eat. (Use a hibachi or an outdoor barbecue.)
4. Broil the eel entrails and add them to the meat, or else simmer them to make soup.
5. Season with salt, pepper, lemon, garlic, or any of the spices you ordinarily use for cooking fish. Or, use one of the fish sauces described elsewhere in this book.

IMPORTANT CHEMICAL ELEMENTS IN SEA FOODS

The formation and utilization of vitamins in our body is often connected with, or even dependent upon, minerals and trace elements — chemical elements that leave only faint traces of their presence in us because they are there in such tiny amounts in comparison to the much larger amounts of other substances around them. Many, but not all, of these trace elements are known for the vital roles they play in our health. Scientists feel quite sure, however, that *all* — not just the clearly understood trace elements — have a place in the maintenance of our health (and so do other people who have a commonsense understanding that the *whole* food cannot always be explained merely by analyzing all of its parts). Such an analysis is difficult, anyway, when the purposes of the parts are still unknown. And we surely do not yet understand the purpose of all of the trace elements in our foods.

Sea foods concentrate trace elements from the seawater around them. This concentration means that a fish or other sea food can contain from a hundred to ten thousand times more of a substance than the seawater arount it contains! Copper, present in fish, sea turtles, and particularly in oysters, in equal or greater amounts than in land meat, is essential for binding iron in the formation of hemoglobin, the red, oxygen-carrying pigment of the blood. The lack of copper can make us anemic even if we have enough iron. (Oysters are rich in iron as well as in copper.) Copper is also believed to extend the effect of insulin, which is activated by zinc.

Tiny amounts of zinc are involved in many other essential body functions, too. Catfish are rich in zinc. In the red snapper, the gills are richest in zinc, followed by the liver, then the milt (or male sexual product). Among the fish, in general, young ones contain more zinc than older ones. Crustaceans and molluscs (especially oysters and octopus) are capable of concentrating large amounts of zinc.

A portion of oysters or other molluscs, crustaceans, or fish roe can provide us with our daily needs, or even more, of cobalt, copper, fluorine, and iodine. Part of the success of fish meal in feeding undernourished populations of the world stems from this power of sea foods to concentrate trace elements, and the need (proven or suspected) we have for many of them.

HOW TO EVALUATE DAILY NUTRITIONAL NEEDS

Although the actual calcium may be ten milligrams in each hundred grams of a fish, and the actual iodine only one-tenth of a milligram in each hundred grams, the fish is really much richer in iodine than it is in calcium. Here is why:

- 10 milligrams of calcium in 100 grams of fish is much less than the recommended 800 milligrams in the daily diet.
- 0.10 milligram of iodine in 100 grams of fish is more than or at least equal to the recommended 0.05 to 0.10 milligram in the daily diet.

Furthermore, there has been (and justifiably so) confusion between *recommended daily allowances* and *minimum daily requirement* for nutrients in our diet. Usually, the recommended allowance is higher than the minimum requirement — just to play it safe, it seems; which all means that we are not at all certain about the roles of some nutrients in human nutrition. This means that our diet should be as broad as possible to cover those hazy areas so we do not suffer from the lack (or indeed surplus) of as yet incompletely understood elements of our foods.

Sea food, by the way, is not a good source of calcium unless you eat the bones, which you can easily do with canned salmon or sardines, and which also provide some phosphorus.

HOW TO TEST FOR MINERALS IN SEA FOODS

You have probably noticed how charcoal is reduced to white or gray ash when burned. Burning removes the black carbon (left when the tree was partially burned to make the charcoal), leaving the mineral salts behind as whitish or gray ash. Besides being a crude test that shows us that the tree contained mineral salts, this ash has curative powers. Fish bones, too, can be reduced to ashes for preparing strengthening remedies. Any ashes you make with this test can be used for the following two remedies.

HOW THE OLD "LEAF DOCTOR" BUILT STRENGTH, IMPROVED DIGESTION AND CIRCULATION

The bone-ash remedy was shown to me by an old Haitian "leaf doctor." I first became aware of the old leaf doctor — *le docteur feuilles* as he was called in French by some of the people he served — one spring night under a waxing moon when he raided my dooryard garden just on the outskirts of a South Florida city. When I surprised him, he did not attempt to escape, but calmly told me that he was a doctor, and that he needed some plants and a fish from my pond for his patients. I nodded my approval and he went off into the night with his booty from my garden and pond. The next time I saw him, early one dawn, he was standing under a tarpaulin lean-to out in an abandoned tomato field, his frail black body bent over a small fire. He was incinerating bones to make bone ash, one of his drugs. (Chemical analysis of some of this ash several days later showed that it contained about 39% calcium and 20% phosphorus...or tricalcium phosphate, a substance recommended by modern medicine as an antacid and as a calcium source in some diseases!)

In time, the leaf doctor took me into his confidence and explained the use of his bone powders. He started with the bones of a freshly slaughtered chicken, field rat or large fish, and carbonized them to make his black powder. To make his white powder, he heated the carbonized powder some more until only a chalky white ash was left.

Several pinches of the black powder daily in water or mixed in food were used to fortify weakened, convalescent or generally ailing persons. The white ash was also supposed to be good for debilitated and convalescent persons, especially those in whom digestion and circulation were poor.

HOW A NORTH CAROLINA FOREST WARDEN STOPPED INDIGESTION

Albert G. occasionally suffered from indigestion during the month-long stays in the North Carolina forests where his wildlife conservation duties took him. Whenever "something he ate" gave him indigestion, he used a Civil War hickory ash remedy to settle his stomach. Albert just poured two quarts of boiling water over a quart of hickory ashes, added a cup of soot scraped from the cauldron hanging over his week-long campfire, and added a handful of carbonized fish bones from his last pan-fried fish dinner. After it cooled and settled, Albert poured off the clearer liquid from the mixture and drank a cupful three or four times during the day until the indigestion stopped, usually in one or two hours. He also told me of a "blood-stopper" his grandmother made from ashes. Albert G.'s grandmother mixed cobwebs with clean soot from way up in the chimney to prepare her blood-stopper, which she sprinkled on minor wounds to staunch bleeding.

IODINE – THE ANTI-GOITER ELEMENT

As you know, migrating saltwater fish, like salmon, return from the sea and swim up rivers to lay their eggs in fresh water. For the strenuous labor of fighting upstream against river currents these fish store up iodine in their bodies.

Completely saltwater or "marine" fish (and crustaceans, too), especially the more active ones, contain the most iodine and are the richest source of that element in our diet. If, however, you need to cut down on iodine, then freshwater fish may be a better choice for you. (It takes six pounds of freshwater fish to supply the same amount of iodine provided by only five ounces of marine fish.)

The skin of fatty fish contains much more iodine than its meat. Lean fish, on the other hand, tend to have more iodine in the meat than in the skin.

A serving of just over three ounces of molluscs or crustaceans, or just under five ounces of sea fish, provides you with as much iodine as you could get from ten full pounds of vegetables or fruit, or from six full pounds of land meat or poultry. Your daily need for iodine (and fluorine, too) can be satisfied by eating sea food twice a week.

FLUORINE – THE ANTI-CAVITY ELEMENT

Sea fish are a good source of fluorine, which protects us against dental cavities. Pacific northwest coast Eskimos (those who still keep to their traditional diet) owe their excellent teeth to their eating of saltwater fish bones, usually several times richer in fluorine than the meat from land animals.

SODIUM AND SALT – HOW TO GET IT AND HOW TO GET RID OF IT

Sodium makes up half of sodium chloride, or salt, which keeps our cells at just the right pressure, preventing them from bursting or from shriveling up. Salt, too, is necessary for our stomach to produce hydrochloric acid, an essential digestive fluid.

Sodium and/or salt is generally found in smaller quantities in freshwater fish than in saltwater ones. Among the saltwater ones, various analyses show that salt and sodium are highest in the cartilaginous fish (sharks, skates, etc.), mackerel, red snapper, lobster, and oysters.

Up to 50% of the sodium and chlorine, or salt, as well as various other minerals in fish can be lost when the fish is boiled or steamed. This loss could be useful to you if you wish to remove as much sodium and/or salt as possible. There is no need, however, for persons on low-sodium diets to worry about salt in fresh fish, because no freshwater and hardly any saltwater fish is rich enough in salt to exceed the permissible amounts in the diets of people whose intake of sodium and/or salt is restricted for various medical reasons. Red meat from land animals, as a matter of fact, may contain more sodium and/or salt than some saltwater fish.

Reserve your caution for when you eat salt-cured fish, canned fish, or when you buy fish that has been kept on salted ice. Chapters 4 and 8 point out how salt is used in the preservation of fish and other fish products. Broiling conserves much of the mineral salts in fish. Deep-frying (which is devilish on digestibility) also conserves minerals, although it may destroy some of the fish's vitamin content. If you like herring, but do not want all the salt that comes with some of them, remove most of the salt like this:

1. Fillet the herring.
2. Soak the fillets in a pan of milk and water (half and half).
3. Drain and dry off the fillets with a clean kitchen towel.
4. Trim off the fins.
5. Cook as desired.

John L., a policeman from Wales, likes his salt cod, but has been told to cut down on his salt. Here is how he has his wife de-salt his cod. She:

1. Washes it off under running water. Sometimes she soaks the salt cod in several changes of fresh, cool water.
2. Cuts it into chunks.
3. Soaks it for twenty-four to thirty-six hours in cold water.
4. Covers it with cold water in a pan or earthenware pot.
5. Heats it until bubbles appear.
6. Skims off the top layer of water.
7. Reduces heat.
8. Covers it.

9. Poaches it for about sixteen minutes.
10. Drains it.
11. Then cooks it according to whatever recipe she is using.

CALCIUM — FOR TEETH, BONES, AND BLOOD CLOTTING

Small whole fish that you can eat with their bones — well-fried smelts, canned sardines and anchovies — are excellent sources of calcium and phosphorus. In whole, larger fish which are boiled, calcium from the bones moves out into the rest of the fish and adds to the calcium content of the meat, although boiling may remove some of the phosphorus content. Marination, too, releases calcium from the bones of larger fish and brings it out into the meat where we can ingest it. The chapters on molluscs, crustaceans, and the safe preparation of sea foods describe ways to pickle and marinate your own sea foods at home.

VITAMIN C AND IODINE FROM A WATERSIDE PLANT

Every vegetable dish in Gina R.'s household contains short-cooked (Oriental style) or rapidly simmered or sauteed watercress (flowers, leaves and stems). When Gina is certain that the streams and wells from which she collects the cress are wholesome and not polluted, she uses the fresh leaves and stems raw in salads and as a sandwich garnish to perk up lagging appetites and to provide vitamin C. (Hence the synonym of "scurvy grass" for certain varieties of watercress; the vitamin C combats scurvy. That is also why the British Navy used to dispense vitamin-C-rich limes to its scurvy-prone sailors on long voyages. So they came to be known as "limeys".)

Along with onions and garlic, various varieties of watercress have quite an iodine content as far as land plants go (seaweeds are richer).

To purify his blood and other body fluids, Gina's husband Dave drinks a weekly cup or two of watercress tea. He makes it by pouring a cup of boiling water over a teaspoonful or so of watercress leaves or powdered, dried root and letting it steep for five minutes; then he strains out the plant particles and drinks the tea while it is still warm.

Dave's German grandfather taught him that fresh cress juice clarifies the voice, helps fight fever and sciatic pains, relieves chest conditions (bronchitis, coughing, asthma), stimulates stomach function and gallbladder secretion, helps lower excess uric acid in the body, alleviates rheumatic pains, relieves gout and protects against stones. Cress is also reported to foster the healing of wounds; for this, crushed foliage and the juices are applied as part of the dressing. Wounds are said to heal more quickly and with less pain when cress is used.

WHAT TO BRING HOME FROM THE BEACH FOR INVIGORATING, HOME-GROWN FOODS

If you are a home vegetable gardener, the sea can help you to grow safer, healthier vegetables. The sea can add nutrients to what you grow if you bring home some "beach manure." Beach manure consists of seaweeds, marine creatures, broken shells, and natural salts evaporated from the sea by the sun. This "manure" is a natural fertilizer that is clean as far as undesirable bacteria and other disease-causing microorganisms are concerned. Beach manure, however, because it completely breaks down into water-soluble substances and gases, does not produce humus — the rich, black soil some gardeners spread over their plants. Yet it brings you a naturally rich, growth-encouraging mix for infusing the nutrients of the sea into your garden or your mineral-loving potted plants without additives or noxious industrial products. The chief contributions of seaweed to your garden are organic matter, bulk for the soil, and mineral salts, although some lavers and other seaweeds also provide ample nitrogenous substances as well.

Seventeen specific seaweeds and other substances from the sea that have been used, and still are, for successful crops and dooryard gardens are:

1. Knotted wrack *(Ascophyllum nodosum)*
   This brown seaweed is also fed to livestock.
2. Bladder wrack *(Fucus vesiculosis)*
   This brown seaweed is particularly good for tightening up loose soils.
3. Kelp *(Alaria, Laminaria,* etc.)
   Whole, dried kelp has proven to be better than the commercial potash that is industrially extracted from it. The whole plant — stems, leaves or fronds, and flotation bladders — not only supplies sodium compounds, phosphorus and other nutrients, but its organic decomposition helps improve the texture and porosity of the soil.

4. Dulse *(Rhodymenia)*
    Dulse is also used to feed livestock.
5. Eelgrass *(Zostera)*
    This is an example of non-alga, waterside plants used as fertilizer.
6. Sponges
7. Sea anemones
    These flower-like animals are rich in nitrogen and phosphorus.
8. Sea cucumbers
9. Starfish
    A hundred pounds of fresh starfish yields about fifty pounds of fertilizer containing about 3% nitrogen and 0.5% of phosphoric acid. Starfish are also used to feed hogs.
10. Coral
    This calcareous material is ground up for carbonates and other minerals which are then added to fertilizers and feeds for animals.
11. Horseshoe crabs
12. Blue crabs
13. Fish
    Whole fish are quite good for nourishing growing plants. Our American Indians showed the founding fathers how to enrich corn plants and encourage healthy growth by placing dead fish around the base of each plant.
14. Shrimp scrap
15. Barnacles
    These crustaceans are dried in the air before being applied to the soil as fertilizer.
16. Oyster, clam and mussel shells
    These mollusc shells are heated and then pulverized. Fresh mussel shells contain about 2% organic matter in addition to the calcium carbonate in them. Pulverized shells are also added to poultry and livestock feeds.
17. Sea mud
    This usually inorganic mineral ooze is layered an inch or so thick over light soil to increase crop yield.

As a home gardener, you can use as fertilizer any uncooked entrail or other parts of any sea foods you eat. Also, you can buy commercially prepared liquid fish fertilizers at garden shops.

3

How to Lose Excess Weight
with Anti-Obesity Sea Foods
and Seashore Activities

FIVE WAYS TO EAT AND RELAX
YOUR EXCESS WEIGHT AWAY

Cecile S. had been a little chubby for years, but she was none-theless attractive and rightly objected to going on any diet just to look "as young as her daughter". When her problem became more serious, however, at 180 pounds, she decided to do something about it. She knew various serious illnesses were associated with real obesity, and was determined to avoid those conditions. Within six-teen weeks after she began a special program, she was down to an appropriate — and attractive — weight for her height and build of 140 pounds.

Cecile S.'s program included many elements which came from the sea, and if you have any sort of "weight problem," you can make use of many of her ideas. She took the following five steps to get herself down to a beautifully natural weight:

1. *Cecile ate lots of low-fat fish.*

   The amount of fat in many kinds of fish is given in the next chapter. The last section of that chapter contains hints on how to select low-fat and high-protein fish.

2. *She seasoned many of her meals with a fat-digesting spice.*
   The cayenne pepper in *seviche* raw fish cocktail is a very good fat digester. Cecile used the recipe given in Chapter 8.

3. *She satisfied her craving for carbohydrates with "anti-obesity" sugars and starches.*
   Cecile discovered that seaweed provides extraordinary starches and sugars, as well as fat-burning iodine to fight excess weight. The nutrients in seaweed are described in Chapters 9 and 10.

4. *She "enjoyed away" weight at the seaside.*
   Hot sand baths, saltwater bathing, the drinking of water, and the seaside climate all gave Cecile the most enjoyable weight-losing vacation she ever had. See Chapter 12 for details.

5. *She "relaxed away" weight at home.*
   Cecile relaxed at home in her own bathroom, and lost some weight doing it. Read Chapters 13 and 14 for ways to bathe, what to put into the bath water, and precautions Cecile took when taking very cold baths to lose weight.

HOW SEAWEED HELPED TO BURN UP EXCESS WEIGHT

Willy B. lived on the Cape, where bladder wrack or kelp ware *(Fucus vesiculosis)* often washed ashore near his home. And that's how Willy successfully lost about 20 pounds of his excess weight. He was certain that the best weight-losing program he ever had and stayed with, was the period of about eight weeks when he drank bladder wrack tea twice a day and smoked "cigarettes" he rolled from dry bladder wrack fronds. Willy's dentist, who often beach-combed with him, thought that the high iodine content of the bladder wrack kept Willy's metabolism hopping along at a high rate, and that's why he lost weight. He warned Willy's cousin, who had an over-active thyroid, not to try this same regimen.

HOW A DIETITIAN SELECTED ROE, FISH, CRUSTACEANS AND MOLLUSCS FOR CALORIES

Lydia S., a dietitian in a large educational institution for the past eighteen years, based her daily menus upon the following caloric values for hundred-gram portions (about three ounces) of roe, fish, crustaceans and molluscs. She emphasized that the way you prepare sea foods may affect calories, such as rich soups and egg-batter-drenched fries. Also, a hundred-gram portion of clam meat alone, for example, is more concentrated in calories than a hundred-gram portion of clam meat plus liquid.

		Calories
Roe	Canned roe from cod, haddock, herring	118
	Baked or broiled roe from cod, shad	126
	Raw roe from carp, cod, haddock, pike, shad	130
	Raw roe from salmon, sturgeon, turbot	207
Bass	Raw black sea bass	93
	Raw white sea bass	98
	Raw smallmouth and largemouth bass	104
	Raw striped bass	105
	Baked/stuffed black sea bass	259
Bluefish	Raw bluefish	117
	Baked/broiled bluefish	159
	Fried bluefish	205
Fish from several species	Canned fish flakes	111
	Cooked fish loaf made with canned flakes	124
	Fried fish made with canned flakes	172
	Cooked frozen fish sticks	176
	Frozen, fried, reheated fish cakes	270
	Flour from whole fish	336
	Flour from filleted fish	398
	(The kind of fish in the above products was not specified by the manufacturers.)	
Halibut	Raw California halibut	97
	Raw Atlantic or Pacific halibut	100
	Raw Greenland halibut	146
	Broiled Atlantic or Pacific halibut	171
	Smoked Atlantic or Pacific halibut	224
Herring	Raw Pacific herring	98
	Solids and liquid of canned herring in tomato sauce	176
	Raw Atlantic herring	176
	Smoked bloaters (smoked whole fat salted herring)	196
	Smoked kippered herring (fat herring split down the back, lightly brined and smoked)	211
	Salted or brined herring	218

	Bismarck pickled herring	223
	Hard smoked herring	300
Ocean Perch	Raw Atlantic ocean perch (redfish)	88
	Raw Pacific ocean perch	95
	Fried Atlantic ocean perch	227
	Frozen, breaded, fried, reheated Atlantic ocean perch.	319
Salmon	Raw pink (humpback) salmon	119
	Salmon rice loaf	122
	Smoked salmon	126
	Solids and liquid of canned chum	139
	Solids and liquid of canned pink (humpback) salmon	141
	Solids and liquid of canned coho (silver) salmon	153
	Solids and liquid of canned sockeye (eye) salmon	171
	Broiled or baked salmon	182
	Solids and liquid of canned raw Atlantic salmon	203
	Solids and liquid of canned chinook (king) salmon	210
	Raw Atlantic salmon	217
	Raw chinook (king) salmon	222
Sardine	Raw Pacific sardine	160
	Solids and liquid of Pacific sardine canned in brine or mustard	196
		196
	Solids and liquid of Pacific sardine canned in tomato sauce	197
	Drained solids of Atlantic sardine canned in oil	203
	Solids and liquid of Atlantic sardine canned in oil	311
Swordfish	Solids and liquid of canned swordfish	102
	Raw swordfish	118
	Broiled swordfish	174
Trout	Raw brook trout	101
	Raw rainbow trout	195
	Canned rainbow trout	209
Tuna	Solids and liquid of tuna canned in water	127
	Raw yellowfin tuna	133
	Raw bluefin tuna	145
	Tuna salad	170
	Albacore (white tuna meat)	177
	Drained solids of tuna canned in oil	197
	Solids and liquid of tuna canned in oil	288

Crab		
	Steamed crab (blue, Dungeness, rock and king)	93
	Canned crab	101
	Crab imperial	147
	Deviled crab	188

Crayfish, crawfish, and lobster		
	Raw crayfish (freshwater)	72
	Raw crawfish (spiny or rock lobster)	72
	Raw Northern lobster	91
	Canned or cooked Northern lobster	95
	Lobster salad	110
	Canned lobster paste	180
	Lobster Newburg	194

Shrimp		
	Cream of shrimp soup (with equal volume of water)	66
	Wet pack (solids and liquid) canned shrimp	80
	Raw shrimp	91
	Cream of shrimp soup (with equal volume of milk)	99
	Drained solids of wet pack canned shrimp	116
	Condensed cream of shrimp soup	133
	Raw, frozen, breaded	139
	Canned shrimp paste	180
	French-fried shrimp	225

Abalone		
	Canned abalone	80
	Raw abalone	98

Clams		
	Canned clam nectar from hard, soft, razor and other clams	19
		19
	Meat and liquid from raw hard or round clams	49
	Solids and liquid from canned hard, soft, razor and other clams	52
	Meat and liquid from raw soft clams	54
	Frozen New England clam chowder made with equal volume of water	54
	Meat from raw hard or round clams	80
	Meat from raw soft clams	82
	Frozen New England clam chowder made with equal volume of milk	86
	Drained solids from canned hard, soft, razor and other clams	98

Condensed frozen New England clam chowder	107
Clam fritters	311

Mussels

Meat and liquid of raw Atlantic and Pacific mussels	66
Meat of raw Atlantic and Pacific mussels	95
Drained solids from canned Pacific mussels	114

Oysters

Frozen oyster stew made with equal volume of water (commercially prepared)	51
Meat from raw Eastern oyster	66
Solids and liquid from canned oysters	76
Frozen oyster stew made with equal volume of milk (commercially prepared)	84
Homemade oyster stew (1 part oyster to 3 parts milk)	86
Meat from raw Pacific and Western oyster	91
Homemade oyster stew (1 part oyster to 2 parts milk)	97
Frozen condensed oyster stew (commercially prepared)	102
Fried oysters	239

Scallops

Raw bay and sea scallops	81
Steamed bay and sea scallops	112
Frozen, breaded, fried, reheated bay and sea scallops	194

Octopus and squid

Raw octopus	73
Raw squid	84

Just as a reminder, note how the preparation method may jack up caloric value. This is due to the added ingredients (eggs, milk, butter, etc.), or to concentration (draining, dry pack) which leaves only the richer solids.

4

Forty-Six Fish to Eat
for Healthful Proportions
of Proteins and Fats

Here are forty-six commercially caught fish and the ways in which they can reach your supermarket or fish market. Some special, appetizing recipes to prepare ocean catfish, codfish, eels, herring, shark steak and sturgeon spinal cord are given in this chapter. More general ways of preparing all fish are explained in Chapter 8.

If you follow a special diet that calls for a certain way of cooking or that limits your use of certain ingredients or seasonings, then also see Chapter 8 for more details on the preparation or curing methods used to get fish ready for market and for the table. This may be helpful in selecting, say, fish that are lowest in salt or some other substance you may wish to avoid.

The owner of a neighborhood fish market in Coral Gables, Florida, told me that he sells over two-hundred kinds of fish and other sea foods every year. To make your shopping for sea food easier, synonyms are given in parentheses after most of the fish described below. Also, protein and fat percentages are given, when available, for most of the fish. This information may help you to select fish on the basis of their protein or fat contribution to your meals. These percentages are quite variable, and depend not only on the condition of the fish and its environment, but also on the laboratory methods used to analyze the fish. Percentages, therefore, should be considered a rough guide only.

ALEWIFE (river herring, rock herring)

- *Clipped roe fish:* Headed alewife with roe left inside.
- *Alewife roe:* Salted, colored as a caviar substitute, and packed in jars as well as canned in brine.
- *Corned alewife:* Gutted, washed, lightly salted and brined, then packed in salt in barrels.
- *Tight pack:* Gutted, cured for at least a week in strong brine, then packed with dry salt in barrels. Also called Virginia cure or hard cure.
- *Vinegar cured:* Whole gutted alewives or fillets.

A hundred grams of raw alewife contain 19.4% protein, 4.9% fat.

A hundred grams of canned alewife (juice plus solids) contain 16.2% protein, 8.0% fat.

ANCHOVIES

- *Salted:* Whole and ungutted, or headed and gutted, fermented four months in salt until anchovy meat reddens.
- *Salted fillets in oil or sauce:* With or without capers, rolled or flat, usually in cans.
- *Canned:* Nothing added, not treated other than canned.
- *Hot smoked and then frozen.*

A hundred grams of processed anchovies contain about 19.2% protein, 10.3% fat. In case you like anchovies but do not want much fat in them, fermented anchovy paste (see Chapter 8) contains about 15% protein, but only 0.4% fat.

ANGLERFISH
(Monkfish, goosefish, abbot, allmouth, fishing frog, frogfish, sea devil)

- *Fresh tails or tail fillets* (because the head is so large!).
- *Frozen fillets.*
- *Hot smoked fillets.*

BARRACUDA (sea or giant pike)
from the Pacific (not the Atlantic, where a Florida expert warned that Atlantic barracuda during some seasons may poison you)

- *Fresh.*
- *Salted:* Headed, split to remove backbone, dry-salted for two days followed by air-drying for several more days.
- *Tempura:* Cakes of barracuda meat and shaved carrots baked in oil and served cold.

A hundred grams of raw Pacific barracuda contain 21.0% protein, 2.6% fat.

BLUEFISH

- *Fresh.*
- *Frozen.*
- *Hot and cold smoked.*

A hundred grams of raw bluefish contain 20.5% protein, 3.3% fat.

BONITO (Atlantic bonito, belted bonito, short finned tunny)

This impersonator may appear as Turkish "tuna fish" in oil, and can even show up (far from recognizable) in garum, the Mediterranean several-month-in-a-pot fish sauce. Pacific bonito has a darker meat and is usually considered suitable only for canning.

A hundred grams of raw bonito contain 24.0% protein, 7.3% fat.

SEA BREAM (porgie)

- *Fresh.*
- *Salted.*
- *Dried.*
- *Canned fillets in their own juices.*

AMERICAN BUTTERFISH
(dollar fish, pumpkin scad, starfish, sheepshead)

- *Frozen.*
- *Smoked:* Whole, ungutted, brined and cold-smoked four hours, then hot-smoked for one hour.

A hundred grams of raw butterfish from northern waters contain 18.1% protein, 10.2% fat; a hundred grams of Gulf butterfish contain 16.2% protein, 2.9% fat.

CARP (This is the classic pond-raised fish produced by fish farmers)

- *Live.*
- *Fresh.*
- *Canned.*
- *Smoked steaks:* Brined then hot-smoked with spices for three hours.

A hundred grams of raw carp contain 18.0% protein, 4.2% fat.

OCEAN CATFISH (wolffish, rockfish, rock turbot, rock salmon, sea cat or wolf, swine fish, sand scar)

- *Fresh cutlets (steaks) and fillets.*
- *Frozen fillets.*
- *Hot smoked.*
- *Dried and boned.*

Sara M., a Manila housewife, dries her catfish like this:

1. Split down the back and clean out organs.
2. Soak overnight in strong brine.
3. Wash well in clean water.
4. Skewer on bamboo splinters.
5. Dry in the sun for about a day.

These dried, skewered catfish hang from Sara's rafters until she needs one or two for her family's dinner.

Although Sara was preparing *ocean* catfish, a mention here of *freshwater* catfish may be of interest. Freshwater catfish, like some other bottom-feeding freshwater fish, may be untasty because of their muddy flavor. The U. S. Department of the Interior reports the following cannery method for removing this muddy taste:

1. Wash well.
2. Remove the head.
3. Cut down the top of the back and along the sides of the backbone to make two fillets (which still contain, however, the rib bones).

4. Make the meat firmer and remove some of the blood by soaking it an hour or two in brine (15% to 20% salt).
5. Steam the fillets ten to fifteen minutes on a rack. The cannery, of course, uses a steamer you would not have. However, perhaps you could steam the fillets some other way, such as in the shellfish steamer described elsewhere in this book.
6. The meat firms up, but the muddy streak stays soft enough to be scrapped out.
7. Flake off the hot meat from the skin and rib bones.
8. Can at 240° F for an hour or an hour and a half, depending on the size of the container in which you are canning the catfish. (Canning is described elsewhere in this book.) Or, carry on from the preceding step and prepare the catfish meat some other way for immediate eating.

COD (Atlantic)

- *Fresh whole, fillets and steaks*
- *Fresh tongues and cheeks.*
- *Frozen:* Whole, fillets, breaded, steaks or other kinds of cuts, raw or precooked.
- *Smoked fillets and steaks:* Sometimes colored.
- *Dried fillets.*
- *Salted fillets or split fish (sometimes deboned).*
- *Salted tongues.*
- *Canned flakes or fillets in sauce or in natural juices.*
- *Canned liver paste.*
- *Brick:* Salted dried pieces pressed together to make one or two pounds.
- *Liver paste sausages.*

PACIFIC COD (gray cod, grayfish)

- *Frozen kneaded masses.*
- *Smoked and seasoned slices.*
- *Salted slices.*
- *Dried.*

A hundred grams of raw cod contain 17.6% protein, 0.3% fat.

If you find codfish too strongly flavored, but like olive oil (and olive oil is really good for you once you develop a taste for it), then try Maria G.'s Portuguese style codfish casserole:

1. Remove all bones from a pound of salt cod and cut the meat into thin strips.
2. Soak the strips of fish in water for twelve hours.
3. Line the bottom of a range-top roasting pan with sliced onions, some parsley and a garlic bud.
4. Layer the strips of cod over the onions.
5. Add a pound of sliced potatoes in a layer over the cod.
6. Sprinkle with pepper and throw in a crushed clove.
7. Pour in enough olive oil to just about cover the cod and vegetables.
8. Simmer in a closed pan, shaking it back and forth occasionally, for about twenty minutes. Then enjoy your Portuguese style cod dinner.

ATLANTIC CROAKER (crocus, hardhead)

- *Fresh whole or fillets.*
- *Frozen whole or fillets.*
- *Cold smoked.*

A hundred grams of raw Atlantic croaker contain 17.8% protein, 2.2% fat.

CUSK (tusk, torsk, brismak, moonfish)

- *Fresh whole or fillets.*
- *Frozen fillets.*
- *Cold-smoked fillets.*
- *Salted and dried.*
- *Canned.*

A hundred grams of raw cusk contain 17.2% protein, 0.2% fat.

DOGFISH (Blue dog, rock salmon)

- *Fresh.*
- *Frozen.*
- *Smoked.*
- *Semi-preserves:* Jellied

A hundred grams of raw dogfish contain 17.6% to 25% protein, 9.0% to 22.5% fat.

EEL

- *Alive.*
- *Fresh whole or fillets.*
- *Frozen whole or fillets.*
- *Aalpricken:* In Germany, gutted small eel, fried and packed in oil.

Eels are not a typically American food, so you may find the following guidelines helpful in handling any live specimens available for use as food. Eel meat is quite nutritious, but its digestibility can be improved by removal of the fatty layer between the skin and the meat. A convenient way of melting away this fat and cooking the eel at the same time, is to slice the unskinned eel (after knocking it over the head with a mallet or rock) and broil the slices until the skin blisters enough to be picked away easily.

It is important to keep the eel alive until the moment you begin to cook it. If you keep your eels alive in a bucket of water (and not a fish pond or holding tank), then change the water often, perhaps every hour or so. Leave the eels in the freshwater for a day or two so they can cleanse themselves out.

If you choose not to broil the unskinned eel as described above, then skin it immediately after it is killed (by clouting it on the head) but before cooking. Skin and cook as follows:

1. Loop a noose around its neck and hang it up.
2. Cut a circle around the eel just below the noose to separate the head skin from the body skin.
3. Take hold of the body skin with a cloth (to keep your fingers from slipping) and pull down as if you were peeling off a stocking; try to do it in one downward tug.
4. Trim fins or any loose ends.
5. Slit along the belly and clean out.
6. Cut off and discard the head.
7. Slice or fillet.
8. Cover.
9. Simmer about twenty minutes at the edge of the burner.
10. Drain, saving liquid.
11. Strain the drained liquid, then pour it over the slices of eel, preferably in a crock or on an earthenware plate.
12. Fry or bake these slices; or cook in any other way you wish.

AMERICAN EEL

- *Hot-smoked fillets or steaks.*
- *Jellied:* Slices boiled in vinegar, salt and spices. Or, slices cooked in brine and gelatine before packing in aspic.
- *Fried and vinegar cured:* Pieces dipped in salt and fried, then soaked in vinegar and spices.
- *Canned:* Smoked, jellied and vinegar-cured pieces.

A hundred grams of raw American eel contain 15.9% to 19.0% protein, 9.1% to 18.3% fat.

FLOUNDERS

- *Fresh whole or fillets.*
- *Frozen whole or fillets.*
- *Hot smoked whole.*

A hundred grams of raw flatfish (flounder, sole, sanddab) contain 16.7% to 22.0% protein, 0.8% to 2.0% fat.

HADDOCK (gibber, pinger, chat)

- *Fresh whole, fillets or steaks.*
- *Frozen whole, fillets, sticks:* Breaded cooked or uncooked, or smoked.
- *Salted.*
- *Rizzared:* Lightly salted overnight, partly dried, then broiled.
- *Vinegar cured:* Brined fillets cooked in vinegar and onions.
- *Canned:* Cooked pieces or flakes in various sauces.
- *Chowder:* Steamed flakes, potatoes, broth (made with salt pork, flour and onion), spices and fish broth.
- *Norwegian fish balls:* Haddock dumplings in bouillon, potato flour, spices.

A hundred grams of raw haddock contain 18.3% protein, 0.1% fat.

HALIBUT (butt)

- *Fresh whole, fillets or steaks (fletches or fliches).*
- *Frozen whole, fillets, steaks.*
- *Frozen cheeks.*
- *Dried:* Brined strips air-dried for several weeks (rackling).
- *Smoked.*

A hundred grams of Atlantic halibut or Pacific halibut contain 20.9% protein, 1.2% fat. Greenland halibut is fatter. Halibut, by the way, has hardly any small bones; so if you are wary of small bones, this fish may be for you. Shark meat, too, will not give you any trouble with bothersome small bones.

HERRING (also see Chapter 8 for how to pickle your own herring)

- *Baked or soused:* Rolled fillets pickled in salt, vinegar and spices, then baked.
- *Bismarck:* Whole or fillets cured in acidified brine, then packed in a weaker acidified brine with onions, carrots, cucumbers, sugar and spices.
- *Bloater:* Whole ungutted fat herring which is then hot-smoked.
- *Bloater paste:* Ground up, mildly smoked salted herring.
- *Bratbuckling:* Small brine-cured and cold-smoked herring that is fried before serving.
- *Cut lunch:* Bite-sized herring bits with skin and bone left on, marinated in wine or vinegar.
- *Kipper(ed):* Fat herring split down the back, brined and smoked.
- *Kaiser Friedrich:* Packed in mustard sauce; also called *mustard herring.*
- *Matje:* Young fat herring with undeveloped (or only slightly developed) sex organs, gutted, roused (mixed with dry salt), lightly cured in salt and sugar, then packed in blood pickle (juices, blood and salt), or in various other ways.
- *Cutlets:* Small chunks of deboned and skinned fillets in tomato, wine, sour cream or other sauces.
- *Herring in jelly:* Cooked and jellied herring with cucumbers, carrots and spices; also called *aspic herring.*
- *Salad:* Diced vinegar-cured fillets of red or white herring; or spice-cured herring with cucumbers, onions, mayonnaise and spices; or so-called *dry herring salad* made with oil or vinegar.
- *Herring in sour cream sauce:* Partly desalted fillets of salted herring marinated in vinegar, with onions, sour and sweet cream, cucumbers, milt (male sexual product that fertilizes roe) and spices.

- *Swedish jellied herring rollmops:* Boneless fillets in red pepper, dill, gelatine, salt, vinegar, and spices.
- *Swedish smoked herring:* Boneless fillets of smoked herring in its own juice, salt, and spices.
- *German herring fillets:* Boneless fillets in crawfish sauce, tomato sauce, milk, wine vinegar, sugar, starch, salt, and spices.
- *German fried herring in mushroom sauce:* Herring fried in soybean oil, vinegar, flour, onions, sugar, salt, mushroom extract, and spices.
- *Herring in wine sauce:* Vinegar-cured fillets in white wine, vinegar with onions, sugar and spices.
- *Red herring:* Whole ungutted herring that is heavily salted and smoked several weeks until hard; also called *hard-smoked herring.*
- *Rollmops:* Marinated fillets rolled around onion or pickle and fastened with a toothpick or clove, and then packed in vinegar, mayonnaise, mustard, horseradish or other sauces.
- *Canned:* A variety of canned products in oil, brine, natural juices and sauces (wine, beer, mustard, lemon, tomato), as well as with vegetables and even fruit.
- *Fresh.*
- *Frozen.*

A hundred grams of raw Atlantic herring contain 17.3% protein, 11.3% fat.

A hundred grams of raw Pacific herring contain 17.5% protein, 2.6% fat.

A NOTE ON NATURAL SAUCES FOR CANNED FISH

A recent letter from a fish cannery (Gunkel Baltamare in Kiel, the capital of the German state of Schleswig-Holstein and principal port of the Baltic inshore fisheries) informed me that their canned herring (made from freshly caught raw fish) are hand-packed, whole fillets in exclusively natural sauces containing one or more of the following: cream, milk, beer, wine, pure vegetable oil, tomato concentrate, onion, cucumber, aromatic spices, mustard, mushrooms, red pepper, horseradish, lobster or lemon. *No preservatives or coloring agents are added,* the firm's director assured me in his letter. In addition to herring and other fish, as well as shellfish, this firm also cans cod livers in the fish's own natural oil, or as a pâté for spreading on toast. Supermarkets in the U. S. carry these northern oceanic products.

MACKEREL

- *Fresh whole or fillets.*
- *Frozen whole or fillets.*
- *Smoked:* Whole hot-smoked; cold-smoked slices in oil prepared as semi-preserves (short-term preservation by protection from light, and mild curing, but not packed under pressure or sealed airtight).
- *Salted:*Whole and fillets pickle-salted, that is, salted in leakproof vats to allow the fish to soak in the pickle (or liquid formed by the fish juice and salt) for several months.
- *Dried.*
- *Canned:* In wine, oil or tomato sauce.
- *Semi-preserved:* Salted fillets cooked in vinegar brine and packed in jars with spices.
- *Paksiw:* In the Phillippines, gutted mackerel soaked in coconut vinegar (made by letting yeast act on coconut milk and mackerel meat), packed with vinegar and seasoning in clay bowls, and simmered thoroughly.

A hundred grams of Atlantic mackerel contain 19.0% protein, 12.2% fat.

A hundred grams of Pacific mackerel contain 21.9% protein, 7.3% fat.

MULLET

- *Fresh.*
- *Smoked.*
- *Salted.*

A hundred grams of raw striped mullet contain 19.6% protein, 6.9% fat.

PILCHARD (large sardines)

- *Fresh.*
- *Frozen fillets.*
- *Smoked kippers.*
- *Salted (pressed pilchard):* Whole dry-salted pilchards packed and compressed into about a third of their normal bulk.
- *Dried.*
- *Canned.*
- *Semi-preserved in vinegar or spices.*
- *Soused:* Pickled in salt, vinegar and spices.

RED DRUM (spotted or channel bass)

- *Fresh.*
- *Salted.*

A hundred grams of raw red drum contain 18.0% protein, 0.4% fat.

RED FISH (ocean perch, bream, Norway haddock, soldier, red perch, red bream, rosefish)

- *Fresh.*
- *Frozen.*
- *Smoked.*
- *Canned:* Pieces in sauces or with rice.

A hundred grams of raw red fish contain 18.0% protein, 1.2% fat.

SAITHE (coalfish, coley, black or green cod, black pollack, rock salmon, Boston bluefish)

- *Fresh.*
- *Frozen.*
- *Smoked.*
- *Salted.*
- *Salted and smoked:* Cured with salt, smoked, then packed in oil.
- *Dried.*
- *Canned fish balls.*

SABLEFISH (black cod, blue cod or coal cod, bluefish, candlefish, coalfish)

- *Fresh.*
- *Frozen.*
- *Smoked:* Called kippered black cod or barbecued Alaska cod.
- *Salted.*

A hundred grams of raw sablefish contain 13.0% protein, 14.9% fat.

SAILFISH

- *Fresh.*
- *Frozen.*
- *Smoked.*

SALMON

- *Fresh.*
- *Frozen.*
- *Smoked:* Especially *lox* (from the German word *Lachs* meaning salmon) from King salmon sides that have been mildly cured: that is, cold-smoked for several days.
- *Salted.*
- *Paste:* Salmon alone or mixed with shrimp or prawn and butter.
- *Fish cakes.*
- *Gravalax:* Swedish-style salmon fillets rubbed with coarse white pepper and sugar, with dill sandwiched in between, and pressed (flesh side against flesh side) on a cold surface for a day.

A hundred grams of raw Atlantic salmon contain 22.5% protein, 13.4% fat (sometimes much less).

CHUM SALMON (dog salmon, calico salmon, fall salmon, keta salmon, qualla, Pacific salmon)

- *Fresh.*
- *Frozen.*
- *Salted.*
- *Smoked.*
- *Air dried.*
- *Fermented:* Pickled chum with boiled rice and salt.
- *Canned.*

A hundred grams of raw chum contain 21.5% protein, 5.0% fat.

CHINOOK SALMON (king salmon, spring salmon, chub salmon, black salmon, tyee)

- *Fresh.*
- *Frozen.*

- *Smoked.*
- *Dried.*
- *Salted.*
- *Canned.*

A hundred grams of raw chinook contain 19.1% protein, 15.6% fat.

COHO SALMON (silver salmon, blueback, Jack salmon, silverside)

Same as for chinook, except that smoking may be by the *Indian-cure* method (beleke, hard-smoked salmon, Indian hard-cured salmon) in which brined strips are smoked hard for two weeks at not over 80° F. Also, coho is hard-salted, whereas chinook is only mildly salted.

A hundred grams of raw coho contain 21.0% protein, 8.0% fat.

SOCKEYE SALMON (red salmon, blueback, quinalt)

- *Canned.*
- *Hard smoked or Indian cured.*

A hundred grams of sockeye contain 20.0% protein, 9.3% fat.

SARDINE (see also pilchard, which is generally the name for large sardines)

- *Fresh.*
- *Frozen.*
- *Salted.*
- *Dried.*
- *Semi-preserved in vinegar and spice.*
- *Canned:* Steamed, grilled, fried in oil, or smoked then packed in tomato sauce or oil (often olive or soya oil).
- *Canned or bottled paste:* Sardine alone; or with pimento or tomato, and sometimes also with butter.

A hundred grams of raw Pacific sardines contain 19.2% protein, 8.6% fat; other sardines go up to 20% fat.

PACIFIC SAURY (mackerel-pike, skipper)

- *Fresh.*
- *Frozen.*
- *Salted.*
- *Dried.*
- *Smoked.*
- *Canned.*
- *Vinegar cured.*

AMERICAN SHAD

- *Fresh.*
- *Smoked.*
- *Canned in its own juice or in oil.*

A hundred grams of raw American shad contain 18.6% protein, 10.0% fat.

SHARK

- *Fresh.*
- *Frozen.*
- *Dried:* In Japan, after salting or broiling; in Iceland, after fermenting.
- *Bone:* Cartilaginous bone is sliced, boiled, and cooled off in water; muscle and hard bone is cleaned off, boiled a second time, and then dried in the sun.
- *Smoked.*
- *Salted.*
- *Pancreas:* A mere one-hundred-thirty sharks can provide as much insulin as four- or five-hundred cattle!
- *Liver oil:* Commercial source of vitamins. In his *Old Man and the Sea,* Ernest Hemingway reported that fishermen drank a cup of shark liver oil every day, and that it was good for colds and the eyes.
- *Fins:* Salted or limed, sun-dried, then boiled as stock to make shark-fin soup. Some Oriental cooks claim that shark fin added to foods promotes vigor and virility.

Like halibut, shark meat will not give you any trouble with small bones. Remember to cook shark slowly and gently to keep it tender.

Molly Q. bought her shark steaks, sometimes along with a chunk of shark liver, at a native Manila market. She found that dry-salted shark meat was best for stew and chowder, but that the brined meat was a bit too strong for her taste.

Molly tenderized her shark steaks by soaking them for awhile — ten or twenty minutes — in fresh lemon juice or vinegar. This precooking soak also got rid of the ammoniacal odor of some shark meat.

Skates or rays are cartilaginous (not bony) fish similar to sharks. Skate "wings" or fins are usually the only parts eaten. Cook these skate fins in salty water and lemon juice, drain, scrape, snip off the bony tips, and then cook them as you would a fish fillet. Poached skate liver, too, is eaten as a delicacy on toast.

SKIPJACK (oceanic bonito, stripe-bellied bonito, striped tuna)

- *Fresh.*
- *Frozen.*
- *Dried.*
- *Canned in oil.*
- *Liver oil:* Rich in vitamin D; the entrails are used to make insulin.

SOLE

- *Fresh.*
- *Frozen.*
- *Canned.*

A hundred grams of raw sole contain 13.0% protein, 1.3% fat.

LEMON SOLE

- *Fresh.*
- *Frozen.*
- *Smoked.*

SPRAT (brisling)

- *Fresh.*
- *Frozen.*
- *Smoked.*

- *Canned:* Smoked or unsmoked, in oil, tomato sauce, chili, mustard, sherry or other sauces.
- *Marinated semi-preserves.*
- *Spice cured.*
- *Paste:* Chopped salted sprats mixed with spices and colored red to differentiate them from sardine paste, then packed in tubes.

STURGEON

- *Fresh.*
- *Frozen.*
- *Smoked.*
- *Canned:* Brined, precooked and packed in its own juice, tomato sauce, aspic, or oil.
- *Semi-preserves:* Pieces dredged in salt, broiled, and packed in wine, vinegar and spices.
- *Isinglass (fishglue, ichthyocolla):* Dried swim-bladder of sturgeon (and also other fish) used in nutritive gelatines. Dried swim-bladders, sometimes salted, are eaten, especially in Canada. See Chapter 10 for swim-bladders as a remedy.

VIZIGA (DRIED SPINAL CORD DELICACY)

Viziga is prepared in Asia, the USSR, Rumania and on the Columbia River in the United States by Chinese people. The Chinese prepare viziga as follows:

1. Remove the head and tail.
2. Pull out enough of the whitish, cylindrical, hollow cord at the tail end until it can be grasped and held with the fingers.
3. Pull out the rest (about four feet).
4. Wash off the blood and slime.
5. Squeeze out the jelly-like material in the cord; or, if the cord is thick enough, split it lengthwise. Discard the jelly-like material.
6. Wash the cord until the wash water is clear.
7. Hang the cord in a current of circulating air.
8. When dry, use it in fish soups and chowders, fish dishes, or even in fish pies.

A hundred grams of raw sturgeon contain 18.1% protein, 1.9% fat.

SWORDFISH (broadbill)

- *Fresh.*
- *Frozen.*
- *Liver:* Used as a commercial source of vitamins.

A hundred grams of raw swordfish contain 19.2% protein, 4.0% fat.

TROUT

- *Fresh.*
- *Frozen.*
- *Smoked.*
- *Canned:* Grilled in butter.
- *Paste:* Smoked.

A hundred grams of raw brook trout contain 19.2% protein, 2.1% fat.

A hundred grams of raw rainbow trout contain 21.5% protein, 11.4% fat.

TUNA

- *Fresh.*
- *Frozen:* Whole, fillets and sausages.
- *Salted.*
- *Dried.*
- *Spice-cured as semi-preserves.*
- *Canned:* Cooked or uncooked, packed in brine, oil, tomato sauce, or aspic jelly. Light meat for canning is from skipjack, bluefin, yellowfin, and especially albacore. Grades of canned tuna are fancy solid pack, standard solid pack, chunk style or bite size, and, finally, grated or shredded pack. Tonno, canned in oil, is more heavily salted than other kinds.

Delicatessen products made from fresh or smoked tuna are tuna loaf, tuna paste, and tuna roll. Tuna sausage made from tuna meat, and also tuna liver, may be cooked and then frozen.

A hundred grams of raw bluefin tuna contain 25.2% protein, 4.1% fat.

A hundred grams of raw yellowfin tuna contain 24.7% protein, 3.0% fat. Other tuna may go up to 18% fat.

Carlotta L., the wife of a Mediterranean fisherman, takes out the intestines and stomach of tuna and other large fish, and makes them into tasty, nutritious fish stew. She:

1. Slits open the stomach and dry-salts it, along with the intestines, for two days.
2. Rinses off the salt.
3. Dries them in the sun.

And to use the dried stomachs and intestines, Carlotta soaks them to soften them up a bit. Then, she either fries them or simmers them with a stew of vegetables and rice.

WALLEYE POLLACK (Alaska pollack)

- *Fresh.*
- *Frozen.*
- *Salted.*
- *Dried.*
- *Spice cured:* Fillets or slices pickled with salt and dregs from rice wine.
- *Liver and entrails:* Commercial source of vitamin-rich oil.

HOW TO SELECT FAT AND PROTEIN FISH

Most fish are low in fat but high in protein. The Pacific cod, carp, flounder, haddock, hake, mullet, ocean perch, pollack, rockfish, and whiting are examples. Hardly any farm animals are that lean. Scallops (which are molluscs) and shrimp (which are crustaceans) are other examples of low-fat, high-protein sea foods.

The Atlantic mackerel, anchovies, herring, salmon, and sardines are examples of medium-fat, high-protein fish. Meat from farm animals is of this kind.

The siscowet lake trout is an example of high-fat, low-protein fish.

The skipjack tuna (especially canned) and halibut are examples of low-fat, very-high-protein fish.

Oysters and clams (both are molluscs), and flounder (in certain seasons when their protein is low), are examples of low-fat, low-protein sea foods.

5

Roe and Caviar for Proteins, and Anti-Diabetic, Anti-Anemia, Anti-Exhaustion Lecithin

Vital forces are locked up in roe and caviar. These highly con-centrated carriers of new life can directly transmit some of their energy to you. All you have to do to benefit from these health-giving sources is to enjoy them as food!

VARIETIES OF ROE AND CAVIAR THAT ARE GOOD FOR IMPROVING RECOVERY FROM ILLNESS

Roe and caviar are the sexual products of fish and other sea creatures. As I prepared to write this chapter, I asked a young Japanese distributor of medical products to tell me something about the sea urchin sexual organs sold in Japan. This young man had some scientific knowledge, and had often eaten sea urchin roe that comes packed in jars. Yet, he was quite shocked when I mentioned them as *sexual organs;* he literally backed off from me, smiling broadly and shaking his head in disbelief. Yet people on the Japanese Islands have eaten them from time immemorial. Here are specific terms for various kinds of these products:

- *Hard roe* (or just roe for short) is the egg mass still enveloped in the ovarian membrane of female fish or various other sea animals.
- *Soft roe (or milt)* is the male sexual product.
- *Black caviar (or just caviar for short)* is made from sturgeon eggs that are sorted for size, washed in cold water, salted, and then ripened before being served. The best caviar, *Malossol,* containing 3% to 4% salt, is a winter product.
- *Grainy (or dry) caviar* is caviar that is packaged as easily separable eggs, and perhaps pasteurized, but without any other preservatives.
- *Pressed caviar* is caviar that is compressed to squeeze out water so that the caviar keeps longer.

Below are specific kinds of roe that are marketed:

- *Alaska pollack roe:* Cured with salt and dyed red.
- *Alewife roe:* Salted, dyed and canned in brine.
- *Carp roe:* The Greeks and others in the Adriatic mix carp or other roe with salt, feta or goat cheese, olive oil and lemon juice for a fully nutritious, non-adulterated meal. (See Chapter 1 for the curative and preventive powers of olive oil and lemons.)
- *Cod roe:* Fresh, boiled, fried, frozen, smoked, salted, made into sausage, or pressed with oil (canned or frozen); also canned with cod liver, salt and spices.
- *Haddock roe:* Fresh, boiled, smoked or canned.
- *Herring roe:* Fresh, frozen, smoked, sun-dried, salted or canned; the Japanese prepare roe by desalting it in fresh water before drying it. Also, they soak herring roe in seawater and wash and dry it before eating it. Or, they soak it in seawater, wash, drain and salt it in either dry salt or brine.
- *Herring milt:* Used to prepare vinegar-cured herring.
- *Mackerel roe:* Canned.
- *Mackerel milt:* Canned.
- *Mullet roe:* Dry-salted, and perhaps also dried and pressed, or salted, pressed and lightly smoked.
- *Saithe or coalfish roe:* Pressed with salt and oil and then frozen or canned.
- *Salmon (or red) caviar:* A substitute for authentic black caviar.

The roe of salmon, as well as that of some other fish, is the commercial source of protamine, a drug used in medicine to counteract the effect of too much heparin (an anticoagulant or anti-clotting substance) so that the blood can once again clot normally. Have no fear, however, that eating protamine-containing salmon roe will cause your blood to clot or coagulate! It won't.

- *Coral (or crustacean roe):* From the soft, greenish-black, egg-laden lobster ovary; it turns red when cooked for eating. The cooked eggs of all edible crustaceans are edible. (Note that the same word — *coral* — is used for crustacean roe and also for the accumulated rock-like constructions of tiny creatures that lead to the formation of immense coral reefs.)
- *Scallop roe:* Yellowish-orange eggs of scallops or pectens.
- *Sea urchin roe:* Fresh, orange-colored egg masses or roe of sea urchins sold in the marketplaces along the coasts in many countries. Italians were observed regularly by a marine biologist as they collected sea urchins along the coast of California, broke open the shells, took out the egg clusters and rinsed them in seawater, and then took them home in jars for eating raw as delicacies. Romans ate sea urchin eggs raw and cooked. In Greece, the piquant, salty-sweet eggs are eaten raw with lemon juice. In Portugal, the whole sea urchin is roasted. The Japanese make a caviar substitute from salted sea urchin eggs.

You may boil a sea urchin in saltwater for about as long as you would boil your breakfast eggs. Then snip the sea urchin open by

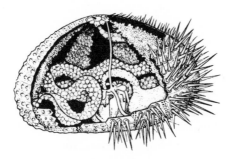

SEA URCHIN

Fig. 1

inserting the point of a pair of scissors into the mouth on the under-side of the shell. Drain. Dip buttered squares of toast or fresh French (or Italian or Cuban) bread into the yellowish cluster of roe and enjoy it.

The eggs of an edible West Indian species of sea urchin, *Tripneustes esculentus*, have caused allergic reactions in some people. Also, Salmonella microorganisms may infest some urchins, and could cause gastrointestinal distress in some people.

Although many species of sea urchins are probably good to eat, my notes indicate only the following nine species as having served as food:

- *Arbacia aequituberculata*
- *Echinometra michelini*
- *Echinus acutus*
- *Loxechinus albus*
- *Paracentrotus lividus*
- *Psammechinus microtuberculatus*
- *Sphaerechinus granularis*
- *Tripneustes esculentus*
- *Tripneustes ventricosus* (the "sea egg")

WHY A DIETITIAN INCLUDED ROE IN DIETS FOR CERTAIN PATIENTS

A dietitian, Lauretta R., convinced the physicians in her hospital to allow her to give roe and caviar to patients whose illnesses had left them weakened and exhausted. Roe and gonads contain more protein and amino acids (though no lysine) than the fish itself, plus vitamin B_1 or thiamine, vitamin B_2 or riboflavin, and perhaps up to 35% lecithin. Lecithin, a phospholipid found naturally in egg yolk, as well as in the brain, nerves and other animal tissues, has been used in fighting the effects of malnutrition, anemia, diabetes, tuberculosis, rickets, indigestion, and nervous prostration. Lauretta R. also pointed out that lecithin, and the roe that contains it, has the power of helping an exhausted person to recover not only from general exhaustion, but also from sexual exhaustion. Lauretta gave caviar and roes of salted and smoked herrings as condiments to her older patients whose digestion needed sparking; such condiments also helped to prevent gas.

HOW A FRENCH COOK PREPARES
EASILY DIGESTED, NUTRIENT-RICH SOFT ROE

François Le C., a French cook in a Mediterranean hotel, rinses the milt or soft roe of carp, herring or mackerel in cool water, strips out any tiny blood vessels from the mass, and prepares it in one of the following ways:

1. Poaches it a few moments in court-bouillon.
2. Poaches it in white wine plus lemon juice.
3. Poaches it in salted water, perhaps natural seawater.
4. Poaches it in a sauce of lemon juice, butter and salt.
5. Rolls the milt in flour and pan-fries it in hot butter.

Pike roe and milt, by the way, may be somewhat poisonous, particularly in late winter and early spring when these fish spawn.

6

Anti-Infective, Anti-Tumor and Nutrient-Rich Molluscs

Enjoy the excitement of dining on the health-bolstering molluscs described in this chapter — a chapter which makes it delicious for you to easily benefit from the anti-infective and nutrient-rich qualities of molluscs. Besides hinged-shell molluscs like oysters and clams, and single-shelled ones like snails, there are also molluscs without any outside shells at all. Octopus, squid and cuttlefish are molluscs, too, but have their shells *inside* them. (The cuttlebone hanging on your canary's cage is the internal shell of a cuttlefish.)

OCTOPUS

Octopus, squid and cuttlefish are all similar in that they have their tentacles or arms attached to their heads. The octopus has eight arms of the same length, but the squid and cuttlefish have ten arms each, two of which are very much longer than the other eight. Octopus and these other animals come large and small, though the smaller ones that fit in your hand are the most convenient and tender ones to cook.

Fresh octopuses are delicious when they are baked in oil, pan-fried, or made into soups and chowders. The Japanese prepare them for market by gutting them, removing the eyes, then drying them in the sun. Octopus semi-preserves are made by first boiling them in water, then marinating them in vinegar. Canned Spanish octopus in soya oil is readily available in most supermarkets.

Here is a general way of preparing tasty octopus chunks:

1. Let the (dead) octopus wash in running water for an hour or more.
2. Beat it with a wooden mallet to soften its leathery flesh.
3. Remove the eyes and beak-like mouth.
4. Cut the meat into chunks and scald or blanch.
5. Drain and wipe the chunks dry.
6. Lightly cook in oil to which chopped onion has been added, along with parsley, garlic and other seasoning according to your own tastes.
7. Add enough dry, white wine and water to just cover the octopus (about two or three cups of wine and two or three cups of water) as the chunks simmer.
8. Simmer in a covered pot until the chunks are tender enough to chew.

SQUID (inkfish, sea arrow, calamar) and CUTTLEFISH (sepia)

Both the squid and the cuttlefish have an internal shell (called a *pen* in the squid and a *cuttlebone* in the cuttlefish). The cuttle-bone has, for a long time, been used as a sort of pumice stone for rubbing ink off of the fingers (back when writing was done with pens that had to be dipped into ink), and as a sort of whetstone against which canaries and other caged birds rub their beaks and on which they nibble. Squid, incidentally, are the largest invertebrates known, and many a whale has been caught that showed the scars caused by the giant suckers of an obviously huge squid that once battled that whale. The ones that we eat, however, are quite small.

These molluscs possess a sac of ink which, although removed by many cooks, can also be used to flavor rice cooked with the meat. (This ink once provided artists with their sepia color.)

Squid and octopus both have horny beaks, but the squid is

probably more apt to bite a careless handler. Take care when picking up large, live squid.

Squid is available fresh, frozen, salted, dried, and canned in oil or in its own ink.

Cuttlefish, considered by some to be less delicate in flavor than squid, are baked in oil, pan-fried, used in chowders and soups, made into ragouts, and used in salads. The dwarf sepia of the Mediterranean is breaded whole or boiled in olive oil; it is also enjoyed in fish soups and salads. Dried cuttlefish for soups is available at Chinese or Japanese grocers in the U.S.

ABALONE
(ormer, ear shell, Venus ear shell, sea ear)

If you do not pull an abalone quickly enough from the rock on which it is attached, it has a chance to clamp down so tightly with its suction-foot that nothing less than a crowbar will loosen its hold. (Clam collectors play somewhat the same game in trying to dig faster than the burrowing clam that they want to catch in time for their clambake.) There are occasional stories of abalone collectors who drown in incoming tides because their fingers get clamped between the abalone shell and the rock on which the abalone is holding. Abalone is marketed:

- *Fresh:* sliced and cooked. Toughness makes it difficult to eat raw, but it can be pounded soft before frying, steaming or cooking in a soup. Or, tenderize it by leaving it (still in its shell) in a refrigerator for two days before preparing it for eating.
- *Dried:* Brined, cooked, smoked, and sun-dried. (Once you soften and cook dried abalone for the table, it is best not to reheat any of it as leftovers later.)
- *Canned:* Brined then minced or chopped into cubes.

CONCHS, LIMPETS, PERIWINKLES, WHELKS

The five-pound *Strombus* conch, the tiny hat-like or knee cap-shaped limpet, the spiralled periwinkle, and the whelk, also spiralled like the periwinkle, all have a common characteristic along with the abalone — they all have a *single* shell. Clams, oysters, mussels, scallops and cockles, on the other hand, all have *two* shell halves hinged together.

The *Strombus* conch is enjoyed in fresh conch chowder by Bahamians, Floridians and many others.

Limpets, once you overcome their snailish tenacity and pull them free from their anchorage on rocks, make tasty and nutritious snacks. Even Wordsworth was acquainted with the strength of these tiny snails, judging from his lines:

> Should the strongest arm endeavor
> The limpet from his rock to sever,
> 'Tis seen its loved support to clasp
> With such tenacity of grasp,
> We wonder that such strength should dwell
> In such a small and simple shell.

Europeans on coastal hikes, if they approach stealthily enough and surprise the limpets before they tighten their hold, pick them up for nutritious raw snacks enroute. The hikers merely bite off the meat from the shell. In France and the Mediterranean world, limpets are cooked in soups, steamed or baked. A biologist watched Italian women collect and eat raw limpets *(Tegula)* from among the seaweed-strewn rocks exposed at low tide at Monterrey, California.

One caution is in order: in a rare case, the radula (rasp-like tongue which the limpet uses to scrape its food from rocks) caused a problem. Many radulae accumulated in the stomach of one avid connoisseur of limpet meat and had to be removed surgically. However, you would have to eat an awful lot of limpets to have that problem.

Periwinkles (also called winkles, but winkles may also mean cockles, which are not single-shelled) are enjoyed in Belgium, France and England after boiling — you need a wire, pin or special fork to snare the meat and pull it out of the shell. I chewed (and finally swallowed, after I mustered the courage) a dozen or so of these snails, and perhaps a few unidentified species that looked like them, that I bought from a street vendor in downtown Brussels. She was boiling them with assorted spices and lemon slices in an enameled dishpan mounted over a heater in her pushcart. (I thought that when in Belgium I had to do as the Belgians do, until I found out that quite a few Belgians, including my own wife who is from Belgium, shuddered at the idea of yanking a snail out of its shell and swallowing it.) Nevertheless, snails, like other molluscs, are nutritious and keep you fortified against winter ills. Supermarkets and gourmet shops sell precooked French snails along with empty, cleaned shells. You simply heat up the snail meats and stuff them into the shells before serving.

The whelk can be bought fresh, semi-preserved (cooked in vinegar and salt) or canned. Fishermen along European coasts sometimes scoop up a mass of whelk eggs — either attached to rocks or floating debris, or washed up on shore and sun-dried into spongy wads — for cleaning their hands.

CLAMS

The largest clam, *Tridacna gigas,* can measure up to about five feet across and weigh up to about 500 pounds. This clam is the one featured in Pacific stories involving "man-catching" clams. One such clam provides a feast for the native community that pulls it ashore. Halves of this greatest of clams are often used as baptismal fonts. There is a smaller, eight-inch version *(Tridacna elongata)* in the Red Sea that also makes a full meal.

There is a multitude of clams, but we can conveniently divide them into two large groups: the *soft-shell clams* and the *hard or round clams.* The soft kind are also called gaper, long clam, long neck, manasose, nanny-nose, old maid, sand clam, sand-gaper, strand-gaper, and squirt clam (because of the little geysers they shoot up when they hurriedly "clam up" and scoot down into the sand when you approach).

The hard or round clams are typified by the quahaug, also called cherrystone or littleneck clams.

Clams are marketed:

- *Alive.*
- *Frozen.*
- *Smoked.*
- *Canned in oil, brine or natural juices.*
- *Canned as soup.*

Clam soups and liquids include the following:

- *Clam chowder:* Made with fried salt pork or bacon, potatoes, spices, onions, clam juice, vegetables, and then cooked; tomato juice or milk is added for cooking.
- *Clam juice:* The undiluted liquid from the clam just when it is pried open.

- *Clam broth:* Diluted clam juice, usually served as a hot broth in cups.
- *Clam nectar:* Clam juice boiled down and evaporated to thicken it.
- *Coquina (or butterfly or wedge shell) broth:* These tiny clams, brilliantly colored with sunset patterns, can be shoveled up, sifted through a screen to remove the sand, and boiled into a delicious, nourishing broth.

Clam juice, or concentrated nectar, bolsters weak and convalescing patients.

Razor clams (so called because they resemble the old-fashioned straight razors that folded into a polished tortoise-shell case) are eaten raw and alive (sometimes with soy sauce, as in East Asia), steamed, baked in hot oil, fried, or in a ragout.

The piddock is a rock-boring clam that is steamed in wine or herbal sauces and eaten, particularly in Italy and parts of France.

A LESSON IN TENSION FROM "UP TIGHT" CLAMS

The sea also provides us with readily usable philosophy. Take the clam, for example, whose habit of getting "up tight" leads to its undoing. The advantage of the clam lies in its protecting itself by closing up tightly to maintain its vital moisture in a dried tidal pool while awaiting the next flood tide, or to ward off being eaten by predators. The clam closes itself so strenuously, however, that it strains its shell to the breaking point. That is why a sea gull can pick up a closed clam, fly up into the air with it, and then crack it open merely by dropping it onto the sand below. A tap from a shovel, too, on the shell of a tightly closed clam down in the sand, can crack it.

Besides reminding us of the consequences of being "up tight," this fact of how a clam tightens up is helpful if you try to pry open a clam or oyster so you can make a meal of it. You have to quickly pick it up and deftly insert a dull-pointed knife (dull-pointed so that it does not stab you if it slips!) between the two shell halves before the clam or oyster realizes that it has to clam up. Or, *with caution,* insert a knife point into a clam's hinge and twist. Be careful not to let the point of the knife glance off and cut you before it drives into the hinge. Then, sweep the blade around so as to cut the muscle holding the meat to the shell. Be sure not to tap the clam or oyster with the knife before you pick it up, for that would make it tighten up even before you tried to open it.

SCALLOPS (Comb shell, fan shell, pecten)

French cuisine has given us the term "escalloped" or "scalloped" (such as "scalloped potatoes") because large scallop shells were used as baking dishes, a custom sometimes imitated by the manufacturers of metal or ceramic cookware who design their vessels as large scallops. I find that sea foods baked or served in real scallop shells, or even in any large clam shell, savor of a quality often lost in ordinary metal utensils. I usually use six-inch shells of the solid surf clam, which is large enough to have served some of our Indians as hoes.

Scallops are marketed:

- *Alive.*
- *Fresh:* Whole or just the large, shell-closing muscle called the "eye" or the "heart" (which is usually the only part eaten).
- *Dried:* Boiled, smouldered and then dried for better keeping qualities. (They are also used as a flavoring ingredient for food.)
- *Canned:* In its own juices, in butter or other sauces.

Although some people have no qualms about swallowing non-personable oysters and clams, they may feel a little differently about the colorful and eye-lined scallop. The inside of the scallop may be any of several shades of red or orange, and it seems to look at you with its dozens of tiny, bright little eyes spots that peer out from within.

COCKLES (heart shells)

Turn a closed cockle so that you can see it from its side, and you will see a definite heart shape, hence its name of heart shell. Cockles are marketed:

- *Alive:* "In Dublin's fair city,
  where the girls are so pretty,
  I first set my eyes on sweet Molly Malone,
  as she wheel'd her wheelbarrow
  through streets broad and narrow,
  crying, Cockles and mussels! Alive, alive oh!"
- *Fresh:* Boiled out of the shells.
- *Salted or brined.*
- *Vinegar-cured (in malt vinegar).*
- *Canned in brine.*

MUSSELS

Although some mussels burrow like clams or even construct nests, most usually gather together in mussel beds, attach to rocks or hang in clusters from pilings.

Mussels are marketed:

- *Alive:* see *Molly Malone* above!
- *Fresh:* Dropped into spiced boiling water containing oil or butter, or cooked (without water) in oil and butter until they gape open.
- *Canned: In various sauces or as a paste.*
- *Semi-preserves:* Brined and seasoned, jellied, marinated; also pickled with onions.
- *Salted.*

Mussels are sometimes eaten raw with lemon juice, but this could be unwise because some of them grow fat from polluted inland waters, rivers and port areas. As a matter of fact, the American Chemical Society reported that outboard motors significantly pollute mussels and oysters because components of the fuel degenerate the gills in these molluscs.

To prepare fresh mussels for the table, scrape any alga or other plant growth off of the shells and rinse them several times in cold water. Discard any open, gaping mussels (because they are likely to be dead and therefore unhealthy). Prepare a kettle of water containing finely minced onions, laurel leaf, parsley, thyme and ground peppercorns (dampened with white wine). Some cooks add about three-quarters of a teaspoon of sodium bicarbonate (baking soda) plus a few capsful of vinegar. This is done as a precaution against possible disease-causing microorganisms that may be present in any undetected unhealthy mussel in the kettle. Affix the lid tightly on the kettle and heat over a hot burner. The mussels should be gaping open in several minutes, indicating that they are ready for the table. Eat heartily, using a two-pronged fork or an empty mussel shell as a scoop. Squeeze a few drops of fresh lemon juice on each mussel before eating, if desired.

OYSTERS

Once oyster larvae settle down and grow into oysters, they stay put; unlike many adult clams, scallops and cockles, which swim, burrow or otherwise get about to hunt for food and to escape their enemies. Another difference between oysters and these other hinged-shell creatures is that oysters build up irregular layers of shell until they look quite irregular and rocky. It is the mother-of-pearl lining on the *inside* of the oyster (and sometimes even a pearl) that makes a collector's item, not its rough-clad exterior. This is just the opposite of the clam's and scallop's allure for shell collectors, who search for the wonderous colors and patterns on the *outside* of the shells of clams and scallops. Some clams, however, may have quite attractive linings, or even pearls in them.

Oysters are marketed:

- *Alive.*
- *Fresh.*
- *Frozen.*
- *Dried.* (Must be soaked one to three days before use.)
- *Smoked and canned in oil.*
- *Semi-preserved in spiced vinegar after cooking.* (Use them to spark up the flavor of many foods.)
- *Canned: Meat, soup, stew, bisque.*

You can make a good oyster stew or soup at home by following these five steps:

1. Take a dozen fresh oysters from their shells and put them, along with their juice, in a saucepan with half a cup of white wine. Canned oysters may be used in place of the fresh oysters if this is more convenient.
2. Bring to a boil, then reduce the heat.
3. Skim off any debris floating on the surface.
4. Add half a cup of fresh cream, three tablespoons of butter, some pepper and any other of your favorite spices (laurel leaf, thyme, etc.).
5. Stir gently a few moments before serving.

Now that you have enjoyed your oyster stew, here are nine easy steps to pickle mussels, clams and oysters at home for a tart treat:

1. Scrub off the shells well.
2. Steam only long enough for the shells to open.
3. Pour the nectar (the juice) into a bowl and save it for Step 6.
4. Take the meat out of the shell and let it cool.
5. Pack the meat with some bay leaves, cloves and lemon slices in sterilized jars.
6. Strain the nectar from Step 3. Let's say you started with a gallon-of shellfish, so you now have about three pints of nectar (if not, add enough saltwater to make that much).

7. Add the nectar to half a pint of vinegar, cloves (½ table-spoon), allspice (½ tablespoon), red pepper (½ tablespoon), and cracked whole mace (outer coat of the nutmeg spice — 1 teaspoon).
8. Simmer forty-five minutes.
9. Cool, pour over the meat, seal, and store in a cool, dark place. (Light tends to darken pickled oysters and mussels.) Let stand about two weeks before eating.

The "R"-month rule: The rule of eating oysters only during months spelled with an "R" originated because oysters are of poorer quality during their spawning period, which occurs when water is warm during the summer, or "R-less" months. Also, transportation used to be safer in cold weather; the oysters were kept unspoiled only until the ice in which they were being shipped melted.

The virtues of the oyster include its delicacy and fine taste, digestibility, and nutritive value. An oyster has been compared nutritionally to a glass of milk.

Nutrients in oysters: A government food chemist, Linton R., grew quite attentive over the years to what his laboratory analyses revealed to him about foods in general, and oysters in particular. He was continually bringing home his enthusiasm for one food or another, but oysters always remained on his must-eat list. His analysis of six oysters on the half shell (about one hundred grams of edible *Ostrea edulis* oyster meat) showed that they contained the following nutrients:

Water	87.1 grams
Protein	6.0 grams
Carbohydrate	3.7 grams
Fat	1.2 grams (containing only 0.23 grams cholesterol)
Chlorine	628 milligrams
Sodium	471 milligrams
Potassium	204 milligrams
Sulfur	180 milligrams
Phosphorus	172 milligrams
Calcium	68 milligrams
Magnesium	39 milligrams
Iron	7.1 milligrams
Copper	3.6 milligrams
Nicotinic acid	1.2 milligrams
Manganese	0.3 milligrams
Vitamin B_2	0.23 milligrams
Vitamin B_1	0.18 milligrams

EIGHT MOLLUSCS
THAT CAN HELP YOU FIGHT INFECTIONS

Molluscs are not only tasty and nutritious sea food, but seem to have the power to protect you against viruses. Scientists sponsored by the U.S. Public Health Service found that extracts of several molluscs were active against an influenza virus. These molluscs included Manila clams, cockle clams, Pacific oysters, abalone, surf clams and northern quahaug or hard clams. The first four were from the west coast of the U.S. and the last two were from New York and Rhode Island. Laboratory studies also showed that two other molluscs — squid and queen conch — inhibited microbes as well as tumors. You can obtain these molluscs in sea food restaurants and fish markets. Keep your eyes open for fresh or canned mollusc juices, too. Be wary, however, when buying a cupful of "fresh" clam juice or soup from such places as fairs and carnivals, where sea food is not an everyday business. Take only a *little* sip at first, and if the taste does not seem to agree with you, then do not drink it. There is an intangible wholesome taste to really fresh clams and oysters that is perceptible even to people who do not ordinarily like sea food.

Fresh abalone juice inhibited poliovirus, *Staphyloccus aureus,* and other organisms that cause disease and infections. Canned abalone juice was effective enough in tests to protect experimental animals from infection with poliovirus.

Although Public Health Service investigators generally found greater *anti-tumor* effect in molluscs that were caught in the summer, the highest concentration of *anti-viral* and *anti-bacterial* activity was found in northern quahaugs or hard clams harvested at Narragansett, Rhode Island, in the *fall and summer*. Other fresh clams, oysters and abalones, as well as the ones specifically tested by scientists sponsored by the U. S. Public Health Service, also may possess some anti-infection powers. The research described above shows that molluscs do have such powers, although those powers vary from place to place or from season to season.

Note: Molluscs are sometimes called *shellfish,* but *shellfish* can also refer to crustaceans, the subject of the next chapter.

7
Crustaceans that Supply Essential Minerals and Non-Fattening Calories

A mouth-watering way to get your essential minerals and non-fattening calories is to satisfy your appetite with steamed or broiled crustaceans. This chapter is meant to help you savor all the health benefits you can get from crustaceans.

BARNACLES

The barnacle, often thought to be a mollusc because of its apparent similarity to snails and other shelled creatures, is really a crustacean and is related to crabs, lobsters and shrimp. In fact, barnacle meat tastes like lobster or crab meat. I once met a Spanish taxi-driver who was sitting by the roadside eating his lunch of steamed barnacles; he sucked out the trunk or stem of each gooseneck barnacle like one does a crab claw, and then split it open to scrape out the remaining meat. Americans (Indians and others) still relish eating the barnacles along our coasts. Some barnacles grow quite large and provide a lot of good meat, like the *picos* barnacle *(Megabalanus psittacus)* on the coast of Chile that grows to about nine inches and is sold fresh or canned. Besides acting as an aphrodisiac to pick up one's interest in life, barnacles, like other shellfish *(shell-fish* means crustaceans as well as molluscs), are rich in minerals. In fact, if you must cut down on certain minerals for some reason but still want to eat sea food, fish, instead of molluscs or crustaceans, may be the answer; perhaps even lake or river fish if ocean fish are still too high in iodine for you. Limpets are also sometimes called barnacles, but that is only because they *look like* acorn barnacles.

CRAWFISH (marine lobster, spiny lobster, rock lobster, spring lobster, langouste)

- *Alive.*
- *Fresh:* Whole or tails, raw or cooked.
- *Frozen.*
- *Canned.*
- *Meal:* Dried and powdered shells, claws, meat scraps, salt, pepper, and other seasoning; used as soup powder.
- *Butter or paste:* Cooked meat or meal and butter fat; used like anchovy paste for spreads, gravies, etc.
- *Soup extract:* Meat, butter, lard, flour, salt, cayenne pepper and seasoning; can also be made with crawfish meal.

CRAYFISH (freshwater lobster)

- *Canned bisque:* Contains crayfish meat, flour, butter and seasoning. Other products are similar to those made from crawfish.

LOBSTER

Crawfish have no claws, crayfish have them; but lobster is so much claw that when you say lobster, many people think of lobster *claw* for dinner rather than a *whole* lobster. An American (or East Coast) lobster has weighed in at 35 pounds, and the huge claws of such an animal account for a quarter or even a half of the creature's total weight! Also on record is a large lobster whose claws made up more than two-thirds of its whole weight. Lobster is available:

- *Alive:* Kept on ice for up to three days.
- *Fresh:* Boiled or steamed.
- *Frozen:* Raw or cooked.

- *Canned:* Cooked in cream sauce, jelly, mayonnaise, its own juices, or prepared as lobster thermidor.
- *Paste:* Canned with cereal and perhaps crab meat.
- *Soup:* Canned bisque, chowder, cream of lobster.
- *Dip (canned).*
- *Meal.*
- *Soup powder.*

NORWAY LOBSTER
(Dublin Bay prawn, langoustine, scampi)

Outgoing fishing boats from the British Isles have sometimes had to ignore fine opportunities to catch Norway lobsters, and have had to wait until the return trip to catch them. This is because these lobsters cannot be kept alive long enough to reach the markets live, but must be boiled just as soon as they are caught. (When dealing with unfamiliar sea animals that you catch for food, your best insurance against poisoning caused by decomposition is getting the *live* animal to where it will be prepared for food as soon as possible. Of course, look out for any stings or bites that you can get from live specimens!) Norway lobster is marketed:

- *Fresh whole or tail:* Cooked or raw.
- *Freeze-dried after cooking.*
- *Frozen:* Raw or cooked and potted in butter.
- *Semi-preserved salads.*
- *Canned: In own juice and brine.*
- *Soup:* Canned bisque.

Although *scampi* is the Italian name for Norway lobster, it also means tail meat dipped in batter and then fried before serving. Shrimp are sometimes sold as scampi.

PRAWNS

Prawn usually means the larger kinds of shrimp, although the two words — prawn and shrimp — are sometimes used interchangeably. Prawn comes:

- *Fresh:* Cooked or raw.
- *Frozen:* Cooked or raw, plain or prepared (cocktail, etc.).
- *Canned:* Cooked or curried.
- *Paste.*

DEEP-WATER PRAWN
(pink shrimp, deep-water red shrimp)

Similar products as for prawns.

SHRIMP (usually brown shrimp, common shrimp)

- *Alive.*
- *Fresh:* Cooked or raw, plain or breaded, whole or tails.
- *Frozen:* Cooked or raw, plain or breaded, whole or tails.
- *Smoked:* Dry or in oil.
- *Dried after cooking:* (Chinese grocers sell these as shrimp chips for snacks.)
- *Salted:* Cooked meat packed with mayonnaise.
- *Canned:* In brine, dry or smoked, shrimp creole, etc.
- *Pasteurized semi-preserved:* Vinegar cured, or in jelly.
- *Paste:* Smoked shrimp alone or with salmon.
- *Soup:* Canned bisque.

Live shrimp should be plunged (while still alive) into boiling seawater, or salted water if real seawater is unavailable. No seasoning is needed, although some cooks may add lemon, pepper or other spices and vegetables. If you use fresh seawater, strain it through cheesecloth to remove any unseen organisms or debris. If you prefer tangy *pickled shrimp,* you can make them right at home by following these five steps:

1. Wash five pounds of fresh, headless, but unshelled shrimp.
2. Prepare the following liquid: water (1 gallon), vinegar (1 pint), salt (2 cups), celery tops (1 bunch), parsley (small bunch), allspice (1 tablespoon), bay leaves (1 tablespoon), red or chili pepper (1 tablespoon), black pepper (1 tablespoon), mace (1 blade), and cloves (½ tablespoon). Boil forty-five minutes.
3. Put the shrimp into the liquid, and boil for another ten minutes.
4. Let the shrimp and liquid cool together.
5. Drain off the liquid and pack the shrimp into convenient containers before refrigerating. Eat them as soon as you like.

CRABS

- *Alive.*
- *Fresh:* Cooked, picked out of the shell and packed ready for use.
- *Dressed:* Cooked white (muscle) meat plus brown (liver and sex organs) meat mixed with cereal or crumbs, spiced and seasoned, and sold fresh or frozen — ready to eat in cleaned-out crab shells; also called deviled or stuffed crab.
- *Canned:* Smoked crab legs, plain, white meat and butter, prepared (crab Newburg, etc.).
- *Soup:* Canned bisque or purée.
- *Paste:* Canned fresh or smoked crab, sometimes with lobster meat.
- *Crab cakes:* Picked white meat, crumbs or cereal, butter, eggs, seasoning, and deep-fried.
- *Hard crabs versus soft crabs:* Soft crabs are hard crabs between molts, That is, a crab is undressed and soft or un-protected while changing from its old, outgrown shell to its new, enlarged shell.

The large claws of some edible crabs are the source of crab meat, not their small bodies. If you take their meat-filled claws for your dinner, but throw the rest of the crab back into the water, it may go right on living and grow new claws (if it survives long enough without its claws for defense against its enemies). As a matter of record, a fisherman did try to market claws from crabs which he returned to the water, but the buying public was apparently suspicious of crab-less claws and his sales dwindled.

HOW TO STEAM-COOK SHELLFISH
FOR EXTRA FLAVOR AND EXTRA WHOLESOMENESS

Crabs, lobster, shrimp, oysters and clams can be prepared quite well merely by dropping them alive into boiling water. On the other hand, there is a certain flavorsome and wholesome extra to be had by cooking these shellfish in steam, according to a Mississippi restauranteur who recommends the following:

1. Fill a fifteen-quart cauldron with three quarts of water. Set a metal or wooden screen or rack above the water in such a

way that the water boils briskly under it, but does not touch the shellfish you are going to lay out on the rack. A tight-fitting lid is also needed.

2. Drop a few lemon slices, some garlic and a diced onion into the water.
3. Lay out your lobsters, clams or oysters in one layer on the rack.
4. Put the lid on the cauldron and let the contents steam about half an hour, depending upon cauldron size, the amount of shellfish, etc.
5. Crawfish, shrimp and crabs take a little less steaming; twenty minutes may be enough. Before steaming, sprinkle these shellfish with salt, cayenne pepper, thyme, etc., or with a commercially prepared crab or lobster seasoning mix.
6. Molluscs, like oysters and clams, gape open when they are cooked. Lobsters and crabs turn red or orange. Shrimp turn pink. These color changes help you to know when cooking is done.

Steamed foods, by the way, are easily digestible and help spark tired appetites (particularly when you have been ill) by intensifying the natural flavor of the food if it is not oversteamed. Try steamed food to help make eating a pleasure again for family and friends who are recuperating from digestive or gastrointestinal illness.

8

How to Safely Buy, Prepare and Serve Sea Foods In Order to Obtain the Benefits of Their Curative and Preventive Powers

Your familiarity with the ways of curing, preserving, preparing and serving sea foods will help you by giving you a better idea of the treatments to which the sea foods in the stores were subjected by the fishing and food industries before reaching you. This can forewarn you about various additives you wish to avoid, say salt if you are on a low-salt diet. Also, knowledge of these methods can guide you in safely enjoying the fresh sea foods you buy or catch yourself.

SEVEN SIGNS OF FRESH, SAFE FISH

A fish merchant I met in a North Sea fish exchange (where boats bring their catches directly from the sea) gave me his seven rules for evaluating the freshness and wholesomeness of fish, assuming that the fish is an edible kind to begin with and not a known poisonous kind. You may readily judge the freshness of fish offered for sale as *fresh* fish (*fresh* fish may be chilled on ice, but not frozen, for then it is classified as *frozen* fish) according to the following seven signs:

1. Fresh fish stare at you with full, clear, bright pupils; stale specimens have sunken and colorless eyes.
2. Fresh fish meat is firm and elastic; stale fish is flabby and no longer stiff and firm.
3. Fresh fish meat under the backbone is pale in color; in stale fish it has a reddish discoloration. Speaking of color, when you get to know how certain fish look when freshly caught, you can judge their freshness by color changes: The green back of a freshly caught anchovy turns dark greenish blue then blackish as the time from capture lengthens.
4. Fresh fish smells "ocean fresh," and certainly not unpleasant; stale fish smells bad, indeed rotten.
5. In fresh fish, the backbone is hard to separate from the meat, chunks sticking on when you attempt to pull the meat off; the meat comes off the backbone of stale fish quite easily.
6. The abdominal walls of fresh fish are firm are resilient; they are soft and pulpy in stale fish.
7. Gills of fresh fish are pink or red, but gray and slimy in stale fish.

Note on slime: Sliminess is often a sign of unwholesomeness, yet some fish are naturally slimy. Slime can be a good sign, for example, on skates (or rays), and can tell you if the skate has been dead less than ten hours. It works like this: wipe off the slime that covers the skate's skin. This slime will *reappear* if the skate has been dead less than about ten hours, but will not appear if the creature has been dead for much longer than ten hours. (Often, however, the skate being offered for sale has already been skinned, and this test of freshness cannot be used.) If you have made the test on an unskinned, unrefrigerated skate, and find that more than ten hours have passed since the skate's demise, and the meat is getting "ripe," it may still make healthful, delicious eating. The degree of "ripeness" or "highness" depends upon the connoisseur eating it and just how strong the odor seems to be. If it smells too strong for you, then do not eat it.

HOW A U.S.A.F. SURVIVAL EXPERT
PREPARED FRESHLY CAUGHT AQUATIC FOOD
FOR SAFE EATING

During exercises in the Panamanian jungle, Sergeant L., a survival expert assigned to the Tropical Survival School of the United States Air Force, gave me some pointers on how to deal safely with unknown fish ana other aquatic animals when preparing them for food. Here are his tips:

1. As soon as you catch a fish, cut out the gills and major blood vessels next to the backbone. Let the fish bleed itself clean. Scale and wash it in clean water. Trout and some other fish do not need to be scaled. Sturgeon and catfish, which do not have any scales, can be skinned.

   The scales of various oily, nutritious ocean fish can be washed off easily without having to scrape them off. Such fish can usually be eaten raw or cooked.

2. To smoke most fish (a technique used to prepare fish so that it may be carried along as people travel), cut off the head and take out the backbone. Spread the fish out and skewer it open with debarked willow or similar branches. Smoke it over a smouldering fire (of willow, birch, cottonwood or alder), but do not let the fish get too hot.

3. To sun-dry fish, hang it from a tree or lay it out on hot stones. Splash the dried meat with seawater to salt it.

4. Marine shellfish (oysters, clams, mussels, crabs and lobsters) often flush themselves clean, to some extent, overnight, if you leave them alive in fresh saltwater.

   Do not eat shellfish that have been collected beyond high tide or those not bathed by tidal water at least 5% of the time. Do not eat from mussel colonies or oyster beds in which you see dead or obviously unhealthy specimens.

5. Although edible sea fish, oysters and clams can usually be eaten raw, you should cook *freshwater* fish, mussels, snails, and crayfish to avoid infection with parasites.

NINETEEN WAYS OF CURING AND PRESERVING FISH

1. *Canned fish* — Canning seals and heats the food long enough to kill or inhibit enzymes and microoganisms, especially *Clostridium botulinum,* the cause of botulism or food poisoning.

2. *Chilled fish* — Fish kept near 32°F but not frozen are still considered to be fresh fish, but may also be called *chilled* or *wet* fish. Fish kept fresh (or chilled or wet) with some pulverized ice at 90% to 95% relative humidity and 32°F to 35°F stay moist, cool and safe for five to twenty days.

3. *Cold storage* — Fish stored below the freezing point (below 0°F) are called *frozen, deep frozen* or *quick frozen* (because the freezing must be done fast enough to preserve quality). Fish frozen at 90% to 95% relative humidity and at −10°F to 0°F stay good for eight to ten months.

4. *Dehydrated fish* — Dehydrated usually means dried enough to prevent growth of bacteria and fungi; that is, less than 25% water stops bacterial action and less than 15% water inhibits the growth of fungi. *Freeze drying,* a form of dehydration, is done under a vacuum with the ice of the already frozen fish sublimating (changing to vapor without first passing through a liquid stage), leaving a finely textured and porous structure that easily takes up water again when being prepared for eating.

5. *Dried salted fish* — Japanese shioboshi is made by drying the fish after it has been soaked in saltwater or dry salt. This is somewhat like, though not completely the same as, *dry* salted fish prepared by piling up split fish in layers separated by dry salt and allowing the juices to drain off. Dry salted herring, for example, is left to cure with dry salt in watertight bins for at least a week, drained off, then packed in boxes with a liberal sprinkling of dry salt.

6. *Fish au naturel* — This is either canned fish cooked in its own juices (as in England), or canned in a light brine, vinegar and seasoning (as in France).

7. *Fish flakes* — Headed and gutted non-fatty fish (cod and haddock, for example) are soaked in brine, steamed, deboned, crumbled into flakes, and then canned.

8. *Fish flour or protein concentrate* — Fish biscuits shark flour bread, fish protein supplement and other details on fish flour appear in Chapter 2.

9. *Fresh fish* — To qualify as fresh, the fish may be chilled but not frozen.

10. *Glazing* — Unwrapped frozen fish are glazed by dipping them in or spraying them with cold water just after they are frozen. This forms a protective film of ice that prevents the fish from drying

out while in cold storage, and undoubtedly also makes an airtight seal that preserves the fish's vitamin content.

11. *Irradiation* — Radioactive isotopes or other sources of radiation are used to kill bacteria responsible for spoilage, permitting a longer shelf life. At 32° F to 68° F, the shelf life is extended by two weeks.

12. *Lutefish* — This is Scandinavian alkaline-cured fish made from *stockfish,* which is gutted and headed fish that has been air-dried hard as a rock. The stockfish is soaked several days in soda and lime solution, then soaked in water for several additional days to wash out the lime. (Lime is calcium oxide, obtainable, among other ways, by burning crushed oyster shells.) Stockfish may be made from haddock, hake, cod and other fish.

13. *Brined fish* have been soaked in salty water. Salt acts as an antiseptic, though it does not destroy all bacteria, and helps dry the fish.

14. *Roused, dredged or rolled fish* have been mixed with dry salt.

15. *Sugar-cured fish* have been preserved with salt plus sugar.

16. *Salt-cured fish* have been treated by one or more of a variety of salting and/or drying methods: soft cure, hard cure, light cure, medium cure, heavy cure, fall cure, Gaspé cure, shore cure, and so on — all referring to the degree of salting and/or the water content of the fish.

17. *Smoked fish* — In its simplest form, smoking can be done by merely hanging the fish — usually in cleaned strips — over a slowly burning fire of wood or peat until the fish is dry, by which time it has acquired a distinctive smoky smell and taste. Commercially, fish may be hot-smoked or cold-smoked. Hot-smoking simultaneously cooks the fish so that it is ready for eating without further preparation. Smoked Greeland halibut, by the way, can be richer in vitamins (B$_2$ and pantothenic acid) than unprocessed fish.

18. *Tinapa* — In the Philippines, fresh whole or gutted fatty fish (herring or oil sardine, for example) are dipped in boiling brine and then smoked.

19. *Tokan-hin* — A Japanese drying method of repeatedly freezing and then thawing fillets, each time progressively withdrawing more moisture from them. (Vitamins are probably lost with the thawing water.)

TWENTY-NINE WAYS
OF PREPARING AND SERVING FISH PRODUCTS

1. *Broiling* — Broil fatty fish to reduce oiliness; no butter or fat is needed. When you broil non-fatty fish, however, add butter or oil to keep it from drying out too much. Broil your well-salted, well-peppered (and well-buttered, if non-fatty) fish on a very hot grill so the skin does not stick.

2. *Poaching* — Never really boil fish, but poach it gently (just below the boiling point) in pre-heated *court-bouillon,* described later in this chapter.

3. *Holding fish together* — Lemon juice or vinegar rubbed over fish before cooking not only increases flavor, color and appearance, but also helps keep the fish from falling apart.

4. *Easy deboning* — Leave the dorsal (back) and ventral (belly) fins on your fish. After cooking, these fins make convenient handles for pulling out the bones attached to them. *Boned* fish, by the way, are only minus their main bones, whereas *boneless* fish are minus *all* their bones, and sometimes skin and other parts as well.

5. *Conserving vitamins* — More vitamins (niacin, riboflavin or B_2, thiamine or B_1) are usually retained in baked than in fried fish, although pan-frying is not as destructive of vitamins as deep frying (by which fish can lose 50% of the above vitamins).

If you do not cook the fish too long and do not use too much water, much of the vitamin content of the fish can be preserved. There are more B-vitamins in dark meat, but dark meat is sometimes removed as inedible while the fish is being processed. Hence, only the white meat reaches the market.

Cook frozen fish without first thawing them out; this preserves flavor and avoids loss of vitamins in the liquid that melts away from the defrosting fish.

6. *Barbecued fish* — You may swear by a charcoal broiled steak, but try freshly caught fish (the Japanese use anchovy, sardine, goby, porgy, or pond smelt) grilled over hot coals or served steaming on a skewer. Pre-boil or toast slices of conger eel, shark or any other fish, skewer them alternatingly with slices of lemon or lime, tomato, cucumber, green pepper, or vitamin-C-rich hot peppers if you have a taste for them, Bermuda onion, and grill it all over a hibachi or barbecue. And, for a special, enzyme-rich treat, you might douse it with a glob of six-month-in-the-pot "ripened" fish

sauce. Details about these powerful, fermented fish products are given towards the end of this chapter.

7. *Caveached fish* — Try sparking a tired appetite with fish prepared like they do in the West Indies. Cut the fish into pieces, fry in oil, pack in earthenware crocks, and then pickle in vinegar, onions, salt and various spices.

8. *Chikuwa* is made in Japan by kneading fish jelly, pasting it around a skewer and then scorching it before eating.

9. *Court-bouillon* is a stock of saltwater, various vegetables, vinegar, seasoning (garlic, onions, thyme, laurel leaf, etc.) and white wine, for cooking fish. Various recipes are readily available in cook books. Or, devise your own court-bouillon to your own taste by experimenting with different vegetables, wines and vinegars (tarragon, malt, wine, etc.). Jean-Pierre, night chef in a Toulouse restaurant, used the following kinds of court-bouillon:

- *For ocean perch, cod, haddock, etc.* — seawater or one and a half teaspoons of kitchen salt in a quart of water.
- *For salmon* — seawater or water and salt, lemon juice, diced onions and carrots, thyme, laurel leaf, pepper.
- *For crabs, lobsters and other crustaceans* — seawater or water and salt, laurel leaf and thyme.
- *For freshwater fish, pike, river trout and carp* — seawater or water and salt, vinegar, diced onions and carrots, thyme, parsley, laurel leaf, pepper. A fine, flavorful and healthful way of cooking a freshwater fish is to plunge it alive, or at least strictly fresh, into this bubbling court-bouillon. Trout as well as other delicate-fleshed freshwater fish cooked in this way take on a bluish tinge, particularly if you squirt some strong vinegar over the fish just before immersing it in the court-bouillon. Serve with melted butter or any white sauce (such as hollandaise) ordinarily used with poached fish.

10. *Cutlet* is a piece of salmon, turbot, halibut, hake or other fish cut at a right angle to the backbone, and including a section of it. Also called block fillet and steak.

11. *Delicatessen fish products* are ready-to-eat tidbits with a limited shelf life, and which may be in one of a variety of sauces, such as mayonnaise, mustard or tomato.

12. *Dressed fish* are scaled, gutted, headed, without tail or fins, and ready for the pan.

13. *Escabeche,* in Spain, is fried fish marinated in vinegar, wine, oil, and seasoning. Watch out for the bones if you buy it ready made (like I have on occasion at Cuban delicatessens in Miami). A detailed recipe is given in the section on pickled fish.

14. *Fillet strips* are sliced parallel to the fish's main bone, and cleaned of fins, principal bones, perhaps the belly flap, and the skin. If the skin is left on, then it may be scaled.

15. *Fish cakes* are patties of fresh or salted fish, crab, lobster or shrimp, potatoes, spices, tomatoes, and onion, dipped in a batter of egg and bread crumbs and then pan-fried or deep-fried.

16. *Fish dumplings* are from non-fatty fish meat (cod or haddock). They are mixed with milk, fish broth and spices, then patted into little balls that are dropped into boiling water or a bubbling soup.

Freshwater fish should be cooked before any tasting is done. This is because they may harbor a transmittible tapeworm parasite (cooking destroys the parasite). Jewish and Scandinavian housewives are particularly prone to infection with fish tapeworms because of their habit of tasting pinches of raw freshwater fish mix (pike, etc.) to assess proper seasoning as they make fish dumplings or *gefilte fish.*

17. *Fish liver paste* is made from salted, smoked or otherwise cured fish or roe ground to a paste and mixed with seasoning, fat or butter. Be cautious, however, about eating livers that may be too high in vitamins A and D, for an overdosage with these vitamins can occur. Lawrence C., a survivor of a torpedoed ship, reported that he became quite ill after eating the liver of a shark he managed to hook (shark liver is very rich in vitamin A). An anthropologist told me that he had the same reaction after eating polar bear liver — also rich in vitamin A. The body oil of fish, however, is a good source of vitamin D at safe concentrations. Herring, mackerel, canned salmon and canned sardines as well as other ocean fish are usually high in vitamin D.

If you take mineral oil as a laxative, by the way, the United States Department of Agriculture recommends that you should take it early in the morning or long enough after a meal so that it does not interfere with your body's utilization of vitamin A and other fat-soluble vitamins (D, E, K) that you take in with your food.

18. *Fish pie* — You have tried chicken, turkey and beef pot-

pies, now try a delectable fish pot-pie. Mix almost any fish with potatoes and vegetables, season to taste, and bake in pastry shells.

19. *Fish salad* — Almost any kind of combination could qualify as a salad. A good basic mix might be diced marinated, salted or boned fish, plus spices, onions, cucumbers, green pepper, vinegar, oil and/or mayonnaise.

20. *Fish soup* — The possibilities are unlimited. The classic fish soup, *bouillabaisse,* is prepared in the south of France by using whatever fish is at hand (eel, scorpionfish or rockfish, and so on), olive oil, white wine, garlic, pepper, saffron, perhaps some molluscs and crustaceans, too, and chunks of fried bread — and much more until it looks more like a fish stew than a soup. Whatever recipe you use, remember that fine French cooks do not let their bouillabaisse cook longer than about fifteen minutes.

A basic fish consommé can be prepared with the following ingredients:

- Fish (1 pound or more)
- Fish bones (6 or 7 ounces)
- Fish head (1)
- Diced onions (1 cup)
- Sliced leek (1)
- Parsley (handful)
- Chopped celery (½ stalk)
- Thyme (tiny pinch) and/or laurel leaf
- Salt (2 tablespoons)
- Water (1 quart)
- White wine (1 cup)

Slowly bring to a boil and keep boiling gently for about forty minutes. Drink a cup of this consommé for an appetizer and use the solid ingredients to make fish croquettes.

21. *Fish sticks or fingers* are cut from frozen *white fish* fillets, breaded and then deep-fried. *White fish* — not *whitefish,* which is a specific fish — is any fish in which most of the fat reserve is in the liver (cod is an example). The opposite of white fish is *fatty fish,* in which the main fat reserve is in the body meat (herring and tuna are examples).

22. *Fish tongues with or without fish cheeks* are sold fresh, frozen or cured in various ways.

23. *Fish wiener or sausage* is fish (often tuna) ground with fat,

seasoning and cereal, then packed into sausage casing. These sausages are then sold fresh, or else pasteurized, canned or smoked.

24. *Fried fish* — Whole small headed and cleaned fish, fillets, steaks, chunks, or even whole "just-as-caught" fish can be deep-fried in oil; olive oil is rich and good for you, but may be too strong if you are unaccustomed to it. Pan-fried fish fillets, steaks and whole small fish need only a pan or skillet, butter and some pepper to make eating a pleasure. A nutritional study, by the way, found that boiling, frying or roasting fish which still contains the liver does not significantly lower the vitamin A content of the oil in the liver.

25. *Fushi-rui and gisukeni condiments* — Fushi-rui is a Japanese soup seasoning made by repeatedly boiling strips of dried fish and then smouldering them until dry. Add pieces to soups and gravies to perk up tired appetites. *Gisukeni* is similar: it is made from baked or boiled small whole fish, soaked in soybean and sugar sauce, then smouldered until dry once again.

26. *Gibbed or gypsied fish* — Although the general term *gutting* is used for eviscerating or drawing fish, *gibbing* and *nobbing* are more specific. Gibbing means removal of gills, long gut and stomach, but not milt or roe, by inserting the knife at the gills. Nobbing is removal of the head and gut by partially cutting off and then pulling away the head along with the attached entrails, but not milt or roe.

27. *Marinated fish* is fish pickled in hot vinegar or acidified brine. The vinegar may be plain or seasoned with herbs or spices, such as allspice. Directions for pickling your own fish are given later in this chapter.

Dried allspice berries (also known as pimento or Jamaica pepper), by the way, are not only used in the flavorful preparation of fish, marinades and pickled foods, but also in baked goods and sausages. Allspice, either chewed or drunk as a tea, promotes appetite and digestion and helps relieve stomachache and painful menstruation. Tea from allspice leaves is a tonic for "good blood" in Jamaica, where a liqueur called *pimenta dram* is drunk for this reason.

28. *Niboshi,* in Japan, is small whole fish or crustaceans boiled or steamed in seawater, then dried in the sun.

29. *Padda sauce* is a tasty, appetite-stimulating fish dip from Malabar, made with butter or oil, chili peppers, mustard and assorted other spices. Dip slices of fish into this sauce either before or after pan-frying them. This sauce can really be considered a *curry.* A

curry — which is not one spice but a whole bag of them — does wonders for glandular function, appetite and body tone.

FIVE ENZYME-RICH FERMENTED FISH SAUCES FOR ACTIVATING CELLULAR METABOLISM

Experience has already shown many of us that sauerkraut that is naturally fermented from cabbage (not artificially created with the addition of acetic acid for instant acidification) promotes digestion, helps clear up furunculosis or boils and other skin conditions, and has even been eaten by diabetics for general improvement in their condition.

The enzymes of microorganisms make this magic of fermentation possible. Bread rises, fruit juices and cereals are magically transformed into wines and beers, cucumbers become pickles, and, primarily in the Orient, sea foods are fermented. (Fermentation is a very important way of preserving food as highly perishable as fish, particularly in countries whose technological capabilities have not yet been developed.) Before sea foods are fermented, they are often salted as a preliminary step. This inhibits the microorganisms that cause spoilage, but does not stop those that cause desirable fermentation.

If you plan to ferment fish that you catch, gut and wash them immediately after catching them to prevent decomposition triggered by powerful enzymes in the gut. In the Far East, however, the whole fish (including the gut) may be left to "ripen" by the action of some of these gut enzymes; the trick is to salt the fish, which lets the "good" microorganisms and their enzymes work but which inhibits the undesirable ones. If you use the entrails, add 15% to 30% of their weight in salt; that is, add fifteen to thirty ounces of salt to a hundred ounces of fish entrails. The Japanese drink rice wine (Saki) along with such fermented fish foods, and perhaps that acts to sort of bolster or protect them from overly "strong" fermented mixes.

The following pastes and sauces will spark your own culinary ingenuity to come up with a good, zesty sauce that tastes delicious, but which smells somewhat milder than some of the six-month-in-the-pot mixes that require heroic conditioning before you can really enjoy the advantages of their full, enzymatically perfected powers.

1. *Anchovy or sprat paste* — Pounded and packed in stone crocks, covered with salt, saltpeter, a few grains of cochineal (red dye made from the dried cochineal beetle), then left to ferment for

half a year. If you do not trust raw anchovy, start with hot-smoked ones. (Hot smoking is done in smoke at 250°F, with a temperature of at least 140°F inside the fish to ensure cooking of the meat.)

This anchovy paste is similar to the Makassar fish, made by the Indonesians from headed and salted anchovies or sprats, rice, yeast and spices. An analysis (published by the Food and Agricultural Organization of the U.N.) showed that this fermented Makassar anchovy paste contained 15% protein and only 0.4% fat, which is much lower than the fat content in fresh anchovies and sprats.

2. *Balbakwa* — In the Philippines, whole fish is packed with salt in a jug and left to ferment for six to eight months. The salt, about three or four ounces per pound of fish, permits the "good" bacteria, not the others, to work during this ripening time. The ripened fish is warmed up a bit in vinegar before serving. (The use of vinegar here is interesting because a farmer from New England once told me that he always took a spoonful or two of vinegar before eating any food he suspected of being tainted!)

3. *Garum sauce* — In the Mediterranean, whole ungutted fish are soaked in heavy brine in stoneware crocks and left exposed to the sun for weeks. The pungent fermented sauce is worth waiting for — once you get used to it.

4. *Nga-bok-chauk*— In Burma, fresh fish chunks are ripened (one can even say allowed to *rot)* before salting and drying in the sun. Enzyme action is fierce, so try only a little bit at a time until you get used to it.

5. *Nuoc-mam* — In Vietnam and Cambodia, whole, small sea or freshwater fish are stacked between layers of salt and seasoning until, months later, the liquefaction caused by enzymatic action is completed, and the *nuoc-mam* sauce is ready.

HOW TO PICKLE YOUR OWN SEA FOODS

Jeanette and Guido H. discovered that they felt in the prime of health (despite being in their sixties) as long as they kept plenty of zesty pickled fish in their weekly diet. After a year of supermarket pickled herring, however, they began to look around for some variety in their pickled sea foods. They soon found a way to pickle their own, and here it is in an easy-to-follow outline.

Herring should be cured for pickling in a special way. Otherwise, if you use regular salted herring, it is not as flavorsome, it's tougher, and it does not keep as long. Cure fresh herring for pickling this way:

1. Cut off the head.
2. Trim off the belly flesh back to the vent (anal opening).
3. Clean well. Take out the kidney (dark streak along the backbone).
4. Wash and drain.
5. Pack loosely in a crock.
6. Cover with brine made with five-eighths of a cup of salt to one quart of water, plus about the same amount of distilled vinegar.
7. Let the herring cure until the salt penetrates into the meat, but remove before the color fades or the skin wrinkles. This curing time is usually about three to seven days, depending upon temperature, the condition of the herring and its size.
8. Repack more tightly.
9. Sprinkle very little dry salt between the layers.
10. Cover with another, weaker brine than that used in Step 6.
11. Store the crock in a cool place until the mixture is used in one of the following recipes, which should be within two or three weeks because this preliminary cure will preserve the herring only for that long.

Cut spiced herring is made by cutting up the vinegar-salt cured herring (prepared in Steps 1 through 11 above) right across the body, making pieces about an inch or inch and a half long, then proceeding as follows (for ten pounds of cut spiced herring):

1. Pack in layers, into a crock, with sliced onion (½ ounce), laurel or bay leaves (2 ounces), whole allspice (3 ounces), mustard seed (2 ounces), whole black pepper (1 ounce), white pepper (1 ounce), red pepper (1 ounce), and cloves (½ ounce).
2. Cover with diluted vinegar (1 quart vinegar plus ½ quart water) and sugar (1 ounce).
3. Let stand at least twenty-four hours in a cool place before eating.
4. Either keep the crock in a cool place, or transfer the herring pieces to glass jars and keep these in the refrigerator. Vinegar, by the way, attacks and destroys the rubber rings in some jar caps, so do not use that kind of cap.

Rollmops, instead of the cut spiced herring, can be made from the vinegar-salt cured herring prepared in Steps 1 through 11. To make the rollmops, cut two fillets from each fish, wrap each fillet around a chunk of pickle or other tidbit (cocktail onion, carrot, baby corn, etc.), fasten each bundle or roll with a toothpick, and pack on end in a crock. Then (for ten pounds of fish):

1. Simmer vinegar (1 quart), sliced onions (½ pound), and sugar (1 ounce) until the onions are soft.
2. Add mustard seed (1 ounce), black pepper (1 ounce), stick cinnamon (1 ounce), ginger (1 ounce), bay leaves (1 ounce), and cloves (½ ounce).
3. Simmer for forty-five minutes from the time the onions turn soft.
4. Cool the liquid and pour it over the rolled herring fillets until they are covered.
5. Let stand about three days before eating.

Potted herring is somewhat pickled, and can be eaten right after cooking it. Jeanette and Guido learned how to pot herring — it works with mackerel, too — in England by the following method:

1. Cut off the head.
2. Clean, wash and drain well.
3. Wipe dry.
4. Rub fine salt and ground black pepper into the belly cavity.
5. Layer into a baking dish, and scatter some bay leaves, allspice, cloves and peppercorns throughout.
6. Add vinegar until the fish is half covered.
7. Bake in a slow oven at 350° F.
8. Cool down and enjoy.

Pickled catfish, carp or other freshwater fish:

1. Clean, skin, and fillet ten pounds of fish.
2. Cut the fillets into two-inch squares.
3. To remove blood, wash the squares in fresh water and soak for sixty minutes in saltwater (a cup of salt in a gallon of water).
4. Drain and pack in a crock.
5. Soak in brine (a gallon of water with as much salt as it will hold in solution) for twelve hours.
6. Rinse in fresh water.
7. Transfer to another crock in layers, interspersed with half a pound of sliced onions and small amounts of white pepper, black peppercorns, red pepper, allspice, mustard seed and bay leaves. Then pour in two quarts of vinegar plus a little over a quart of water.

8. Bring to a gentle boil and cook until you can pass a fork easily into the fish.
9. Cool, add some more spices, onion and lemon slices and pack into glass jars, adding the cooking liquid after straining it.

Escabeche can be made from pickled mackerel, kingfish, corvina, or tuna. In fact, you can try quite a few fish and get a good *escabeche;* soft-fleshed fish, however, do not seem to turn out so nicely. Here is a successful way of making it:

1. Cut ten pounds of fish up into bite-sized pieces.
2. Wash and drain the pieces.
3. Soak in brine (one gallon of water with as much salt as it holds in solution) for half an hour.
4. Wipe each piece dry.
5. Prepare a pint of olive oil, minced garlic, some bay leaves, and several red peppers in a frying pan.
6. Cook the pieces of fish (in the oil prepared in step 5) until golden brown.
7. Let the fish cool.
8. While the fish is cooling, add sliced onions to the oil and cook until they are yellow. Then add black peppercorns (1 tablespoon), marjoram (½ tablespoon), cumin seed (½ tablespoon), and vinegar (1 quart) to the oil (don't let it splatter on you!). Cook slowly for about twenty minutes or so. Cool.
9. Pack the fish pieces into sterilized jars, with some bay leaves and red peppers, and cover with the cooled liquid made in Step 8. Close at once. Wait twenty-four hours before eating. Although it is not a good idea to keep it more than three to six weeks (depending upon how cool it is kept), it gains somewhat in flavor after a few weeks.

Seviche (fish marinated in citrus juice):

1. Select ten pounds of fresh, firm-fleshed ocean fish, such as corvina, striped bass, weakfish (sea trout). Or use mussels (remove the beard), shrimp and crayfish (that is, freshwater lobster), or even raw clams (remove the dark blob or stomach).
3. Wash and drain.
4. Mix diced fish or shellfish with five thinly sliced onions, three cloves of pounded garlic, salt, a dozen sliced yellow

chili peppers, five cups of sour-orange juice or lime juice, a dash or two of cayenne pepper.

5. Let stand overnight. The *seviche* will then be ready to eat, and will keep about a week or longer if kept refrigerated.

HOW TO CAN YOUR OWN HEALTH-PACKED FISH

Inlanders who would like to store up good fish, perhaps after a fishing trip to the ocean or perhaps to benefit from favorite health-packed fish with which commercial canneries do not bother, may do their own canning. Here are the guidelines Yvonne L. obtained from the U.S. Department of the Interior, and which she followed for successful canning of many kinds of fish right in her own kitchen. These government guidelines were used in tests which determined processing time and temperature, flavor, softening of the bones and texture of the meat. If the bones of a particular fish were not softened after two hours of cooking at 240° F, or after an hour and a half at 250° F, then any further tests for that fish were stopped. The barracuda, for example, was tested as follows:

Processing		Flavor after 1½ hours at 240°F, but before canning	Bone	Meat texture	How packed	Taste after canning
Time	Temperature					
1½ hrs.	240°F	Good	Soft	Good	Spiced-plain	Good
1 hr.	250°F	Good	Soft	Good	Smoked-tomato	Delicious

Remember, however, the warning earlier in this book about Pacific barracuda being safer to eat than the Atlantic species.

Softened and disintegrated bones, of course, liberate calcium and phosphorus to bolster your nutritional intake.

The home canning method Yvonne learned from the government's testing program was:

1. Scale the fish and remove the head, tail, fins and insides.
2. Wash well.
3. Cut into a convenient size to fit your jars.
4. Soak sixty minutes in a 5% brine solution (50 grams of salt in 1 quart of water).

5. Pack the fish into jars.
6. Set the open jars down into a large kettle of even weaker brine (half the strength of the brine in Step 5) and boil for fifteen minutes.
7. Invert the jars on wire or plastic mesh, or a screen, so that they can drain completely without the fish falling out.
8. Add several bay leaves and a slice of onion to each jar, seal at once.
9. Heat for one-hundred minutes at a temperature of 240°F.

A modification of the above method was simply that hot tomato sauce was poured in to within half an inch of the top of the jar immediately before the jar was sealed. The tomato sauce was made with:

1. Tomato puree (2 quarts).
2. Sugar (2 tablespoons).
3. Finely diced onion (half).
4. Spiced sauce (4 tablespoons) made by simmering the following ingredients for an hour (then straining out the solids): vinegar (1 quart), water (1 quart), sugar (4 ounces), whole black pepper (1 tablespoon), bay leaves (4), sliced onion (1), marjoram (1 teaspoon), mustard seed (½ tablespoon), cloves (½ tablespoon), crushed cardamon (½ tablespoon), and ginger (2 tablespoons).

A small word of caution: Yvonne already had some experience in home canning with fruits and vegetables; so she was familiar with the smooth operation of a pressure cooker — a kettle that lets you cook food at a temperature higher than the usual 212°F (boiling point of water at sea level), thus destroying most of the microorganisms that might ruin your home-canned foods. For safety and good results, follow the instructions for canning given by the manufacturer of your own particular pressure cooker. In general, care for the safety valve on your pressure cooker (according to the manufacturer's instructions) after each canning session, and have the pressure gauge checked for accuracy every year (or sooner if you use it frequently). Happy and delicious canning!

NOTES ON SPICES USED IN PICKLING AND CANNING

Cardamon has been used as a tea to improve digestion, neutralize stomach acidity, alleviate cramps and expel gas.

Cloves are astringent and antiseptic, and have been used in various ways for toothache, stimulation of stomach function, soothing nerves and toning up the blood vessels.

Ginger has been used to increase the flow of digestive juices and to stimulate the appetite, relieve constipation (but also used by some people to stop diarrhea, too!), expel gas, and fight bad breath. Essence or oil of ginger has been taken (a teaspoonful for adults, fifteen to thirty drops for children), diluted with hot water, for relieving intestinal cramps and expelling gas.

Marjoram has been used in various ways (as a spice in foods, as a tea, as a wet dressing, etc.) to relieve migraine and other headaches, spasms, epileptic attacks, pain of neuralgia, colds and sniffles, eye inflammation, scorpion stings, disordered menses, facial twitching and drunkeness. Marjoram is said to strengthen the stomach, help tone up the nerves, expel gas and foster the flow of urine. A typical recipe is three to five grams of the powdered flowering plant steeped as a tea for toning up the stomach or as a liniment to rub on painful rheumatic spots.

Powdered mustard seed has been used as follows:

1. Teaspoonful taken three times a day for dyspepsia (impaired digestion).
2. Two teaspoonsful taken in a glass of hot water to cause vomiting (to clear out certain kinds of poisons that have been swallowed).
3. Plaster, poultice or pack (half mustard and half flour) to alleviate neuritic and rheumatic pains and to improve circulation. (Take care to stop application short of really burning or blistering the skin.)
4. Tea (made from three grams of powdered seed) for colds, bronchitis, and improvement of circulation.
5. Bath to reduce fever.

Pepper, in tiny amounts, stimulates the stomach and digestion, is a good fat-digester, stimulates the kidneys and helps glandular activity in general.

Cinnamon has been used to improve stomach function, to control diarrhea and vomiting, to reduce an overly abundant menstrual flow, and to counter acid stomach. A tea is made from cinnamon in the same way that it is made from many of the other spices — by pouring a cup of boiling water over a teaspoonful or so of the spice and letting it steep awhile. How to make other teas is covered in detail later in this book.

AVAILABILITY OF TURTLE PRODUCTS
THAT PROVIDE PROTEIN, ENERGY-RICH FATS
AND MIRACULOUS CURING POWERS

Besides the curative powers of turtles, which are described in Chapter 10, these animals make a healthfully delicious meal. You can buy turtle:

- *Fresh:* Meat from loggerhead turtles and green turtles is washed in brine and hung up overnight before being used as steak or soup meat.
- *Frozen:* Especially turtle steaks.
- *Canned:* Soup, flippers, meat, stew.
- *Dried:* Especially fat belly flesh of the green turtle.
- *Smoked.*
- *Shell:* As soup stock.
- *Soup:* From shell, or from dried and/or smoked fat belly flesh of the green turtle.
- *Eggs:* Especially unripe eggs of the green turtle.

Recipe for turtle bouillon: Claude L., a diesel engine mechanic who traveled about the Florida Keys making "boat calls" to fix broken engines, kept himself well nourished with frequent helpings of turtle-shell soup made as follows: scald off the horny layer and boil the bone until the cooking liquid thickens, then ladle a portion of it into a bowl of turtle-meat bouillon prepared as any other beef bouillon. If the turtle taste is too strong, you can boil up beef bone instead of the shell, and use portions of that in the turtle bouillon to cut the full, ocean-rich flavor. Claude L. also made free use of turtle oil for clearing up an occasional skin rash and for protecting himself from excess sun and the moist, salt air of the Florida Keys. (Sea turtles may be under strict government protection in some areas, so check first before collecting them!)

Take caution with snapping turtles: The largest of freshwater turtles, the snapping turtle, is often the chief ingredient of a fine soup. It can grow to about three feet and weigh up to 200 pounds. There are several problems, however, associated with this turtle. One problem is the number of parasites in wild specimens, and the other is the snapping part of the snapping turtle — its jaws. And, the snapping jaws are backed up by a quick temper. I once picked up a snapping turtle from the bank of a small pond in northern New Jersey and put it on the floor of my Volkswagen, behind the driver's seat, to take home to my children. No sooner had I driven fifty feet than I heard (really *felt*) a hiss in my ear and a scraping on the back of my seat. The turtle had reared up on its hind legs and lunged at my head, barely missing me. The jaws of a large specimen can bite a pencil in half or mutilate a finger. Use heavy gloves and keep clear of the jaws when handling large turtles.

9

Seaweeds and Other Algae for Minerals, Vitamins and Renewed Vigor

THE UNIQUE FOOD VALUE
OF SEAWEEDS AND OTHER ALGAE

Marine algae, commonly called seaweeds, are tasty, nutritive foods that have kept survivors of shipwrecks and ditched aircraft alive and well until rescue. They have fed nations of people since their histories began, and still feed many people in today's world. A Japanese distributor of medical equipment, on a training visit in Miami for several months, courteously offered to let me taste the dried red seaweed his mother mailed to him from his home in Japan. (Just like the New York Jewish mother who mailed her son, who was stationed with the U. S. Army in Europe, a lovingly wrapped package of kosher salami...covered with green mold after its two-month transAtlantic crossing. Or, like the Italian mama who likewise lovingly shipped off a gallon jar of homemade meat raviolis to her son aboard a U. S. submarine in the Pacific Ocean!)

Seaweeds provide us with abundant iodine, vitamin C, proteins and other nutrients. In seawater, many minerals may be so dilute that we cannot use them directly as food. But we can use the mineral-laden seaweeds that accumulate and concentrate these traces of minerals in their cells.

The unique contribution of seaweeds to human nutrition, and your health in particular, may well be this concentrating power, along with the presence in them of certain polysaccharides found only in seaweeds. (Cellulose and starch are examples of polysaccharides found in flowering land plants as well as in some seaweeds. Polysaccharides found *only* in seaweeds include alginic acid, laminaran, fucoidan agar, and carrageenan.) Nutritional science and medicine are just beginning to uncover the startling benefits of some of these substances, many of them still too experimental to describe in detail.

HOW SEAMAN E. SKIMMED UP
A BALANCED DIET WITH SILK STOCKINGS

The crew that navigated the Kon-Tiki from Peru to Polynesia in 1947 successfully ate raw and cooked plankton as an experiment in living from the sea. Plankton is a wonderously rich assortment of drifting plant and animal life — much of it microscopic in size — that abounds even in the apparently transparent water of the open sea. It is part of what gives the ocean water its living quality that cannot be imitated in the laboratory or in a marine aquarium. A fine mesh net drawn through the water behind a ship accumulates a brownish-green film or scum of this plankton, and this is what the Kon-Tiki sailors ate.

Although many creatures, both tiny and gigantic (like whales), feed on nutritious plankton, we find it more convenient and much more palatable to derive our own nutrition by eating the fish that eat the plankton, or by eating the predatory fish that eat the vegetarian fish that feed on plankton. But, ultimately, plankton nourishes us at some point along this food chain — in the same way that we derive essential nutrients from the milk of a cow that eats grass.

Seaman E., who was shipwrecked on a tiny, lava-strewn island in the Pacific Ocean, salvaged a case of silk stockings, a dory equipped with an outboard motor, some fuel, and the clothes on his back. He caught only one fish during his first two days of being shipwrecked. Necessity, the mother of invention, soon inspired him to run the dory in circles around the tiny island, dragging a string of silk stockings behind him. A planktonic film built up in the fine mesh of the stockings. With some fuel-drenched pieces of flotsam and sparks he generated from the motor, Seaman E. cooked and ate his planktonic catch every day for the next four days, when, fortunately, he was rescued — none the worse for his experience in surviving "off the fat of the land." (He was lucky, perhaps, in that he did not collect a possibly poisonous bloom on the water, such as the "red tide," which occasionally poisons fish in Florida waters. Other experimenters, however, have not always been as fortunate in living on plankton.)

SELECTION OF SEAWEED FOR SAFE EATING

Select seaweeds that are still attached by their holdfasts (holdfasts are like roots that only hold, but do not transport nutrients to the plants as the roots of land plants do) to rocks or other seaweeds. Or select seaweeds that are floating in the sea or in the surf, or a least still bathed by the same tide that brought them up on the shore. Fully beached seaweeds may be too decayed to eat. Seaweeds are grayish-white when dead; however, dead-*looking* seaweeds that still retain their color may well recover their healthy appearance once the tide bathes them again.

SAFE, PALATABLE PREPARATION
OF SEAWEED FOODS

Various cooking and preparation methods have already been described for some seaweeds. Here are two ways of preparing any edible seaweed:

1. Dry the delicate kinds of seaweed in an oven, over a barbecue pan, or in the sun until they are crisp. Then, break them up and add them to hot water to make soup, or use them as a seasoning in clam or other broths.

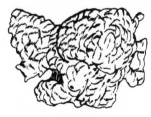

GELATINOUS

BLUE-GREEN
COLONIES
SPREAD OVER
GROUND IN
GRASSY MEADOWS

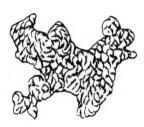

Fig. 2

2. After washing, soften the thick, leathery kinds of seaweeds by boiling them before adding to soups or stews, or eating them as you would eat spinach.

FRESHWATER ALGAE AS HEALTHY FOOD

Besides the seaweeds (that is, the algae that grow in the sea), there are algae that grow elsewhere. In nutritional research carried out for space exploration operations, a freshwater alga *(Chlorella)* was found to be almost a complete food in itself, containing about 50% protein with all the essential amino acids (except the sulfur-containing ones), fats, carbohydrates and most of the vitamins and minerals needed by human beings. Tests in Japan showed that three or four ounces of dried Chlorella added to noodles, soup, green tea and baked goods did not affect the taste or appearance of these foods.

Space exploration research, however, merely confirms what people have known traditionally for hundreds and even thousands of years. The Aztecs, who inhabited Mexico City when it was called Tenochtitlan, were avid eaters of blue-green alga. When the Spaniards came, they ate it, too, according to the accounts of the *conquistador* Hernando Cortez, the historian Prescott and many others.

Contemporary desert nomads of the Sahara, too, traditionally know the value of alga. A Belgian Trans-Saharan Expedition reported that *dihe,* which is sold as a flat cake made almost entirely of a blue-green alga *(Spirulina platensis),* was quite rich in proteins.

Another blue-green, freshwater alga *(Nostoc)* is found on moist ground as green, marble-sized blobs of jelly. Wash and dry these gelatinous blobs, and use them in soups and broths.

In clinical experiments, volunteers were able to eat algae *(Scenedesmus obliquus* and *Chlorella pyrenoidosa)* as their main source of protein for twenty days, without suffering any ill effects.

A VITAMIN-RICH GREEN SEAWEED SALAD TO RELIEVE DISCOMFORT

Sea lettuce is a bright green, translucent seaweed whose wide leaves or fronds are like the thinnest of plastic sheeting that covers your clothes when they return from the dry cleaner. It contains vitamin A, some of the B group vitamins, vitamin C, and has been eaten by people to relieve gout as well as made into appetizing sea salads for stimulating tired appetites. Ralph Y., a New Jersey coastal hotel manager, kept his gout from acting up by eating sea lettuce raw like land lettuce, mixed with mayonnaise, salad dressing, lemon juice, or vinegar and oil.

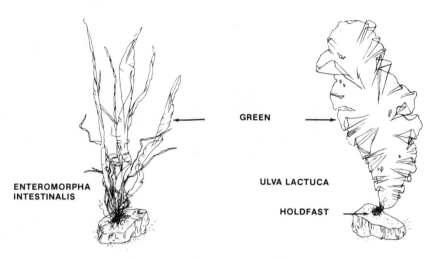

Fig. 3

BROWN SEAWEED: SEA SUGAR
AND SEA STARCH FOR A NEW TWIST

If ordinary sugars from land plants disagree with you, then perhaps the marine equivalent of those sugars, mannitol in the young stalks of sugar wrack or tang, will be better for your system. Likewise, if you find that ordinary land-grown starches do not agree with you, then perhaps the marine equivalent of those starches, laminaria in kelp, is better for you. These are available in many health food stores.

Edible kelp is richest in iodine during the late fall and winter; drifting kelp tends to lose some of its iodine. Soften kelp by boiling, then add to other foods or eat it alone like spinach. Kelp stems and flotation bladders (that help the kelp to float close enough to the surface to utilize sunlight) are sliced, desalted by soaking in several changes of fresh water, and candied...and that's a lot of candy, for some kelps may grow to over one-hundred feet in length. Kelp broth is made in a proportion of one to ten, that is, one bowl (or cup or quart) of fresh or dried kelp to ten bowls (or cups or quarts) of

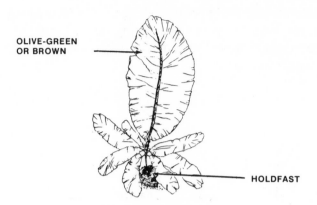

OLIVE-GREEN
OR BROWN

HOLDFAST

KELP (ALARIA SPECIES)
Laminaria and other kinds of brown seaweeds may
also be called kelp.

Fig. 4

water. First soak the kelp four hours in the water, then bring it all to a boil.

Alaria, a kelp of cool and cold waters, contains vitamin B_1, vitamin C, potassium, calcium and iodine (if you collect it before the rain leaches it out).

Sugar tang, or wrack, is roasted, candied, used for sweetening soups and rice, and making salads.

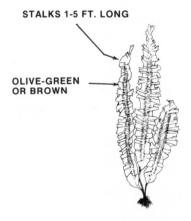

STALKS 1-5 FT. LONG

OLIVE-GREEN
OR BROWN

Fig. 5

Another brown seaweed, sea cabbage, has been canned with vegetables and tomato sauce, as well as with mussels and rice.

RED SEAWEED: A SEA-RICH VEGETABLE FOOD

Tough, rubbery-looking carragheen or Irish moss shrinks and becomes crispy when dried, and tender when you boil it. Eat it as side dish.

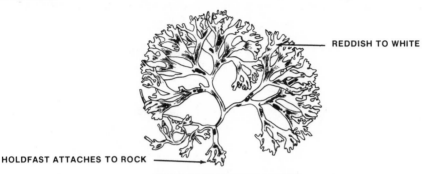

REDDISH TO WHITE

HOLDFAST ATTACHES TO ROCK

CARRAGHEEN (IRISH MOSS)

Fig 6.

In Japan, red seaweed, in general, is roasted until the reddish-brown turns green, then it is used to spice up soups and gravies, or eaten as a vegetable. The Japanese sun-dry it until it breaks up easily, then they break off chunks to toast over an open fire.

Prepare laver *(Porphyra)* by boiling with a dash of vinegar until it turns gelatinous; cool, form into patties, dip in oatmeal, flour or cornmeal and fry. Or, you can chew on it for water if you get thirsty but do not want to fill up on too many liquids for some reason. (New Zealand troops quenched their thirst this way during the World War II.)

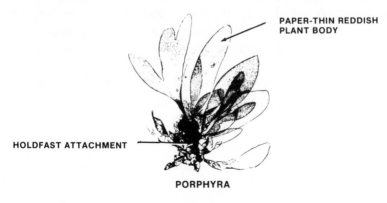

PAPER-THIN REDDISH PLANT BODY

HOLDFAST ATTACHMENT

PORPHYRA

Fig. 7

Dulse *(Rhodymenia)*, another red seaweed, is quite well known in the British Isles and especially Scotland. It contains carbohydrates, proteins, the amino acid proline, vitamin C and minerals. Dulse was known on this side of the Atlantic, too, for Longfellow has John Alden standing on the Plymouth shore and calling out:

> Welcome, O Wind of the East, from the
> caves of the misty Atlantic,
> Blowing o'er fields of dulse and the
> measureless meadows of sea grass.

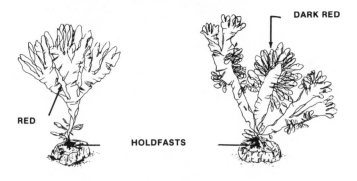

PULSE (RHODYMENIA)

Fig. 8

Dulse is leathery before you cook it, tastes sweet, and you can even use it as chewing tobacco once you dry and roll it. In Norway, it was boiled in milk to make a soothing soup.

Some red algae, when boiled and then cooled down, form the agar-agar (or agar for short) so useful to bacteriologists, who grow microorganisms on it, and to people who make ice-cream, jellies and other foods that require gelatine. Agar also provides you with dietary bulk without irritating the lining of your gastrointestinal tract.

The next chapter goes into more detail on how you can benefit from the medicinal value of seaweeds.

10

Oceanic Medicine Chest
of Curatives and Preventives

HOW PENGUINS ILLUSTRATE THAT SEA FOOD HEALS

Antarctic penguins were found to be bacteriologically clean — virtually no bacteria in them — because their diet included krill (tiny, shrimp-like crustaceans) which, in turn, had fed on a marine alga or seaweed. An antibiotic was eventually isolated from that alga and later patented as a drug! Likewise, many of the sea foods described in this book can provide curative and preventive effects, even though these foods are eaten for enjoyment and not taken just as medicine.

You can obtain important health benefits by keeping a sort of "medicine chest of helpful aquatic products," as well as by eating fresh sea foods. This chapter points out some of the first-aid remedies that are available not only directly from the seashore, but that can also be purchased from drug stores, herbal shops, health food stores or distributors that deal in sea foods.

HOW TO REDUCE
STOMACH ACIDITY WITH SEA PRODUCTS

How a fisherman soothed acid stomach with earstones: In a cavity behind the brain of the plaice (a flounder-like fish) are several limy "stones" or concretions of calcium and other minerals. Harry L., a British fisherman, used these earstones to alleviate his gastric hyperacidity while at sea. He simply ground the limy, chalky stones to a powder and dissolved it in a cup of warm tea to swallow it better. He obtained relief within the hour — much sooner, he said, than with commercial antacids. Other fish, and also lobsters, have earstones, and Harry believed that they would work just as well as the plaice earstones. One of the two earstones I cut out from a large grouper head is illustrated below.

How a lighthouse keeper used crawfish as an antacid: Lou S., a New England lighthouse keeper, pulled crawfish out from under the rocks around his lighthouse, scraped the carbonate and phosphate concretions from their shells, and powdered them for use as an antacid whenever he suffered from excess gastric acidity or heartburn. (*Crawfish* and *crayfish* often refer to either marine or freshwater lobsters. The preferred usage, however, is crawfish for marine species of clawless lobsters and crayfish for freshwater species of tiny-clawed lobsters.) A pinch or two of the powder in a glass of warm water usually subdued Lou's acid stomach.

How a perfumer used snail operculum as an antacid: An operculum is the "door" which a snail pulls up and closes after it withdraws into its shell. Carl H., a perfumer, was well aware that snail opercula (plural of operculum) were burned as incense in India, that persons suffering from epilepsy and hysteria inhaled the incense

AN EARSTONE FROM A LARGE FISH

Fig. 9

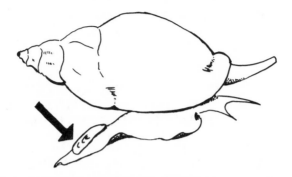

OPERCULUM ON THE FOOT OF A WHELK

Fig. 10

to treat themselves, that the substance was taken by mouth for liver conditions, as well as rubbed with oil on the skin for various skin irritations, and, also that snail opercula were burned as incense in the Temple of Jerusalem (as reported in Exodus 30: 34-36). Carl was so impressed with all this information that he tried snail opercula instead of his usual antacid tablets. It worked. Several pinches of ground-up opercula (from the group called *Turbinidae,* which includes turban shells) a day relieved his acid stomach. The following figure illustrates a snail operculum:

Note of Caution: In the Pacific and Indian oceans, certain cone shells (that is, the *molluscs* living *inside* the shells) can inflict painful and even lethal stings. So be careful when collecting in those places, or in the tanks of friends who keep exotic species of sea life at home.

How coral relieved excess stomach acidity: Corals are generally known because of their calcium-rich, condominium-like homes which they build by extracting minerals from the sea around them. Not all corals are stony; some may be leathery, horny or even spongy. A local government official on a Pacific island took tiny pinches of roasted-and-then-crushed jeweler's coral as an antacid to neutralize his excess stomach acidity after overly sumptuous official dinners. He also reported that he saw New Guineans sprinkle coral powder into bleeding wounds to staunch the flow of blood and initiate clotting.

Coral is found strewn over many beaches, and can also be purchased at shell or gift shops. Be certain, however, that any coral you purchase has not been sprayed or otherwise treated with varnishes, etc. If you collect *living* coral from a reef, remember that the animals that reside in the pores of the stone-like structure are related to jellyfish and anemones...and some can sting you. Vinegar and olive oil soothe your skin if you do get stung.

WHAT CHRISTOPHER COLUMBUS
AND THE PASTEUR INSTITUTE IN PARIS
LEARNED ABOUT TURTLE OIL

You can give yourself a protective skin treatment with turtle oil. Christopher Columbus reported that Portuguese sailors treated their leprosy and other skin conditions with turtle oil from the Cape Verde Islands. Experiments at the Pasteur Institute in Paris, France, indicated that turtle oil was indeed effective on artificially induced leprosy in rats. Emiliano S., a plantation overseer on a Caribbean island, also found turtle oil helpful. From time to time he went down to the seacoast to buy turtle oil from coastal villagers, who caught the large marine turtles that swam offshore and boiled down their meat for oil (they simply skimmed off the oil from the top of the boiling water). Emiliano rubbed the oil into the many minor skin irritations that plagued him and his men who worked the plantation. The oil not only relieved itching and burning skin, but also seemed to actually heal it. Their use of turtle oil also protected them from insect stings and bites, and from the burning rays of the sun. Fish markets or authorized turtle fishermen can supply you with enough fatty turtle meat to make all the turtle oil you need.

HOW LOUISIANA CAJUNS ALLEVIATED
DISCOMFORT WITH ALLIGATOR TONGUE OIL

Alligator tongue oil, long used by the Cajuns in Louisiana to soothe the "miseries," is reported to alleviate, at least temporarily, arthritic and rheumatic pains and to relieve asthma. This effect may be due to the same action that causes profuse perspiration in people who take the oil, or it may be related in some other way to the steroid effect found in it by pharmacologists at Xavier University in Louisiana. Alligator tongue oil can be separated from alligator tongue that is simmered over a low fire. Skim the oil from the surface of the water. A teaspoon or two of the oil seems to have been a good dosage in most cases, bringing an end to discomfort in less than an hour. Alligator tongues can be bought from alligator hunters (in areas where hunting is allowed), or from zoos when old or injured gators are put to sleep.

HOW A FIFTY-FIVE-YEAR-OLD LADY PHARMACIST KEPT HER SKIN WRINKLE-FREE

A wrinkle-free, fifty-five-year-old lady pharmacist, Clara R., gave me the following three reasons why she always insisted on turtle oil for her own skin care:

1. It permeates the skin well.
2. Her skin (and the skin of many others she knows who use turtle oil) tolerates it perfectly.
3. It is mildly astringent and tightens up loose skin.

Clara noticed a definite improvement within a few weeks of her first use of turtle oil, and now applies it periodically to keep her skin clear and attractive.

Turtle oil, as a matter of fact, is used in the cosmetic industry (and not just by Clara) as a vehicle or carrier of fat-soluble vitamins (vitamins A, D, H, K), lecithin and cholesterol. It can be bought as a pure, vitamin-enriched oil, or as an emulsion (oil droplets suspended in water) in many beauty-aid shops.

EFFECTIVE SUBSTITUTES FOR COD LIVER OIL

A Miami Beach retiree, Jake S., was well aware of the value of vitamin-rich cod-liver oil — his mother had spooned plenty of it into him to supply him with vitamins A and D as he grew up. So, when he began to suffer from the health problems of his advancing age, he decided to try cod-liver oil again; he relieved his painful rheumatism and chronic skin irritation by rubbing the oil well into his skin. Jake claimed, too, that his grandmother rubbed cod-liver oil into her mammary tumor for relief from discomfort. When Jake's favorite pharmacy ran out of cod-liver oil (he had bought out their whole supply), he tried the only other oil on the shelves — turtle oil. It worked just fine.

A missionary who spent many years in the Seychelles and in India reported that people there took spoonfuls of turtle oil just as cod-liver oil used to be taken here, that is, to prevent rickets, to alleviate lung conditions, and as a tonic (especially for anemia).

HOW A RAILROADER REMOVED SPOTS
FROM HIS EYEBALLS

You should try to obtain a supply of pike-liver oil for your oceanic medicine chest. Rudo W., an elderly, retired railroader who once worked the trans-Siberian line (that ran near the lakes from which he fished for pike), used pike-liver oil to remove spots from his cornea. Rudo cooked the pike liver gently until its oil rose to the surface of the water. Then he daubed it on spots he wanted to clear up, like corneal flecks (perhaps caused by his locomotive's hot cinders); he used it daily for a week or so until they lightened and disappeared. When Rudo no longer had time for fishing, he began to buy the pike liver fresh from the market, where fish merchants saved the livers for him.

SIX KINDS OF FISH A NORWEGIAN FISHERMAN
USED TO RELIEVE HIS CONSTIPATION

Lars P., a Norwegian fisherman, often suffered from constipation, brought on by long hours of work without sufficient sleep or regular mealtimes. He was always able to relieve his worst cases of constipation within two hours by eating a soup made from fish stomachs and swim-bladders, dried in the wind and the sun's warmth (but in the shade, *not* in direct sunlight). Lars said that the best fish from which to take stomach and swim-bladder were croaker or drum, meagre, queenfish, weakfish, silver perch, and spot. Some Chinese food distributors in the U.S. carry dried fish stomachs.

HOW AN ITALIAN FISHERMAN ALLEVIATED
ABDOMINAL COMPLAINTS
WITH FLOWER-LIKE SEA ANEMONES

You can stop some pains in your abdomen with sea anemones. Sea anemones are flower-like animals related to jellyfish and corals. Their gracefully ondulating ring of tentacles is arranged like the petals of a multi-colored flower. The colors of the beadlet anemone, for eample, may be brown, deep red, green-speckled red, and bright green, with a line of blue dots at the base of the tentacles! Mario L. told me that the people of an Italian village ate sea anemones (in winter rather than in the summer) because they promoted the flow of urine, helped digestion (especially after heavy meals), and controlled diarrhea, as well as flushed out bladder stones. The villagers cooked the sea anemones in wine and ate them to achieve these benefits, but Mario said he himself ate his sea anemones raw on bread as a snack when he was out fishing, and that they always cleared up his stomach and helped his digestion. He only ate one species called oplet or snake-locks *(Anemonia sulcata)*, and warned me that another kind *(Sagartia elegans)*, used as bait to kill rodents, was not be be used for food or any remedy. A fish vendor in the marketplace where Mario traded told me that sea anemones could be used to remove unwanted hair, and that his wife rubbed a mashed-up fresh anemone on her legs several times a week to remove superfluous hair.

Check with local fishermen or vendors of fish first before eating any anemone, as some species may be unwholesome, such as the one mentioned above as a rat poison.

HOW A FLORIDA SCHOOL TEACHER
RELIED ON SEA URCHINS FOR HEALTH

Sara L., who grew up as a missionary doctor's daughter, relied on her accumulated knowledge of medical lore when she began to teach school in the rural areas of Florida and in out-of-the-way places in the Florida Keys. Sea urchin eggs are not only tasty raw or cooked but are highly nutritious, and Sara ate them to promote the flow of her milk when she was nursing her children, to promote her urinary flow, aid her digestion, strengthen an occasional case of weak stomach, and to loosen her bowels when constipation troubled her.

Sara made sea urchin ashes from the shells, and sometimes also included the spines as well, to apply to minor cuts and wounds where the iodine from the shell acted antiseptically. When she made ashes, Sara took care to roast the shell only until the first ashes were produced, but not enough to whiten them. Sea urchin ashes also helped alleviate scabies when she rubbed them over the affected areas of her students' skin. Ashes, just as the raw or cooked animal, promoted urinary flow; two pinches dissolved in a glass of warm milk worked fine. Incidentally, Sara's grandfather told her that sea urchin ashes rubbed into the scalp promote the growth of hair. Sea urchins or their shells can be picked up on both the Atlantic and the Pacific coasts of North America.

Note of Caution: Take care when handling sea urchins that are still covered with their spines; fine tips of these spines may break off under your skin and fester, or else make it painful, until they work themselves out again. The reef-dwelling, poisonous long-spined (as long as 16 inches) *Diadema antillarum* should not be used. Young urchins of this kind have banded spines, and adults have black or dark purple ones.

A FOOD HEALS AND PROTECTS ONLY IF YOU NEED IT

Your body *selects* what it needs from a sea food, whether it be a healing power, protection from disease or resistance to infection. There should be no misgivings about eating those foods just for enjoyment; that is, do not be afraid that the medicinal power of the food will be too much for you if you are not ill and are not looking for a remedy. If a sea food increases or decreases blood pressure, loosens up constipation or prevents blood clots from forming, it usually does it in people whose bodies need those effects. Take, for example, vitamins. Although too much of certain vitamins may sometimes cause a rash or other sign of an overdose, the usual situation is for the healthy body to simply ignore extra vitamins, or perhaps store some up to assure continued resistance to any unexpected infection or stress that may come along. And, in fact, many substances (such as some vitamins) are considered *protectors* rather than curers. People who eat, say, oysters or seaweed regularly are rarely, if at all, subject to diseases like goiter. Eating regularly, of course, means as part of your whole menu, not exclusively oysters and seaweed.

HOW A SPONGE DIVER BENEFITED
FROM THE ANTI-INFECTIVE POWERS OF SPONGE

Sponges are animals despite their plant-like appearance. Until most sponges are processed to remove the tiny, sharp fragments imbedded in them, they are not soft enough for scrubbing your back in the bath. This roughness, however, was what made them useful to Georgios E., a sponge diver from the Florida west coast. Georgios used them to clean out minor wounds, sometimes even after the wounds got infected. The abrasion and iodine content seemed to speed up healing.

When his throat was sore from a cold or flu-like infection, Georgios burned dry sponges in an ashtray near his easy chair, where he relaxed as he breathed in some of the vapors. "It's antiseptic, and it works for me" Georgios said. "Take a pinch of roasted and powdered sponge, dissolve it in a glass of warm water, or even in a glass of warm muscatel wine, and gargle with it to clear up laryngitis overnight. It's like painting your throat with iodine, like people used to do before antibiotics came along." A few sponges burn and blister your skin if you touch them while they are still alive. For example, in Florida waters there is a bright orange sponge and a mahogany-brown one that should be avoided.

HOW A MEDITERRANEAN FISHERMAN USED STARFISH FOR FIRST-AID

An Italian fisherman, Luciano R., not only ate raw starfish gonads (sexual organs and roe) as a delicacy, but also ate boiled starfish as a general antidote against unwholesome foods (that he was forced to eat at some parties) and to promote his digestion when he felt indisposed. I was somewhat skeptical at first when Luciano told me that his father rubbed crushed starfish into his bald spots to encourage the growth of hair; yet, on second thought, it did not seem too illogical, considering that fresh gonads of sea animals are indeed hormonally powerful.

For spider and scorpion bites and stings, Luciano's village friends cut open a live starfish and held the cut surface against the wound; this seemed to neutralize the venom, or at least lessened the pain and swelling following such bites and stings.

Luciano's grandfather, who often suffered from the effects of too much alcohol, was usually helped to recover by doses of powdered starfish dissolved in a glass of wine cut with water. Also, the village epileptic was given powdered starfish in wine to drink, or else was induced to inhale the vapors of burning, dried starfish. Both of these remedies appeared to calm down the violence of the epileptic attacks, Luciano assured me.

HOW AN AGED CHILEAN PHARMACIST USED A WHALE PRODUCT TO ALLEVIATE ACHES

Gerardo P., a ninety-year-old Chilean pharmacist who had many friends among the sailors and ship captains who once plied the Pacific coasts of his country, used ambergris to reduce the aches and discomforts of his advancing years. Ambergris, a lump of waxy substance from the intestines of sperm whales, is occasionally found floating in the ocean. Gerardo, whose supply of ambergris came from his seafaring friends who had been whalers, learned about ambergris by reading what a French lawyer and gastronome of the eighteenth century wrote:

> ...when I have one of those days when the weight of age makes itself felt—a painful thought—or when I feel oppressed by some unknown force, I add a glob of ambergris the size of a bean, pounded with sugar, to a cup of strong chocolate, and I always find my condition improving marvellously. The burden of life lightens, thought flows easily, and I no longer suffer from insomnia. ...

Gerardo had no trouble in finding ambergris. If you find it difficult, however, you could try writing to a perfume manufacturer where ambergris is used to make perfumes.

HOW SEA SNAKES ALLEVIATED RHEUMATISM

If you suffer from rheumatism, you might find a liquid made from sea snakes helpful. Chan W., an engineering professor who learned Chinese medical lore from his Chinese parents, relieved his rheumatism with two kinds of sea snakes *(Hydrophis cyanocinctus* and *Polamydrus platurus)* which he first washed and then immersed in a jug of either red or white wine. He drank the wine several weeks later, and also rubbed it into parts of his body that were affected by rheumatic pains. When Chan had the time, he dried a freshly decapitated sea snake (one of the two kinds whose scientific names appear above) in the sun, boiled it in wine or vinegar, and then drank the liquid (if it was wine), or rubbed it (if it was vinegar) on the painful spot.

Chan's successful remedy may not be as far-fetched or superstitious as it may seem, if we realize that venomous creatures have yielded valuable painkillers to modern science on many occasions. The tincture made of a whole sea snake in wine or vinegar could well contain an active, painkilling ingredient from the snake's venom. The venom certainly calms down the snake's prey when injected by the snake's fangs, but does not hurt the snake when it swallows the prey. Many a first-aider has sucked out rattlesnake or copperhead venom from a victim's wound, and as long as the first-aider did not have any cuts in his mouth or on his lips, the venom was harmlessly destroyed in his digestive tract. Chan W. found that his rheumatism always relented within a few hours after one-half a cup of his snake tincture was either rubbed on (if it was the vinegar kind) or drunk (if it was the wine kind).

HOW A RURAL SCANDINAVIAN NURSE
RELIED ON SEAWEED FOR ALL-PURPOSE REMEDIES

Conserving the iodine content of seaweed: You should certainly have some seaweed in your oceanic "medicine chest." The isolated fisherman and farming families of the region served by Ingeborg K., a nurse, benefited from her knowledge of the powers of seaweed, a readily available food and remedy literally scattered over their doorsteps. When the iodine content of the seaweed was important, Ingeborg recommended that her patients collect fresh seaweed from the shoreline or rocks at the water's edge before any rain fell on it, otherwise the fresh water would wash out much of the iodine in the seaweed. (See Chapter 9 for details on the safe selection of seaweeds from the beach.)

Tonic soups and salads from seaweed: Ingeborg recommended red seaweeds for tonic soups and salads to alleviate the discomfort of lung and other chest ailments, irritating coughs and gastrointestinal irritations. She also used red seaweeds to help prevent peptic ulcers and to reduce the risk of blood clots in her patients who were prone to suffer from thrombosis. (Scientific studies have shown that certain seaweeds do indeed possess anti-clotting properties.)

If your seashore guide book gives scientific names, then select *Gracilaria, Chondrus,* and *Gigartina* for the above-mentioned tonic soups and salads. You can obtain these seaweeds from the international distributors listed in Chapter 15, and also from natural sources.

Agar for gastrointestinal distress: To loosen up her own constipation (resulting from her irregular diet and hours of sleepless travel throughout her extensive territory), Ingeborg took agar, yet also used it to soothe the irritation caused by diarrhea. To make agar, she boiled the red seaweeds mentioned above, then cooled down the liquid until it set like a gelatine. When she did not have time to collect her own fresh seaweeds, she bought powdered agar at a pharmacy and boiled it just like she did the fresh seaweeds. A few tablespoons of agar gelatine usually alleviated her gastrointestinal distress. (In the U.S., Chinese and Japanese grocers carry dried agar strips that have to be soaked soft before use.)

Mineral-rich tonic seaweed mixture: Ingeborg also bought Corsican or worm moss (a mixture of *Alsidium helminthochorton* plus other seaweeds) from village apothecaries, but did not tell her patients to eat it to expel intestinal worms (as most others who bought it did). Instead, she recommended it to her convalescing patients who were recovering from tuberculosis. They seemed to recuperate more rapidly, possibly because of this seaweed mix's high mineral content (especially iodine and bromine) and tonic qualities.

Kelp tea, poultice, cigarettes, salads and soups: Bladder wrack or kelp ware *(Fucus vesiculosis)* went into one of Ingeborg's favorite teas (and was also sold in tablets in health food stores and apothecary shops in town) to alleviate gout and to use as a poultice on aching muscles and various skin irritations. For reducing weight, bladder wrack was prepared as a tea, and also rolled into cigarettes for smoking. For goiter, this seaweed was often eaten along with tangle *(Laminaria)* in salads or drunk as a tea. For providing vitamins and minerals in the diet of undernourished children and convalescing adults, bladder wrack plus tangle stems were eaten in salads and soups. Health food stores and some pharmacies carry kelp tablets as well as dried kelp itself.

Be cautious about taking kelp tablets if you suffer from acne. A U.S. medical journal reported that kelp tablets seemed to aggravate existing acne in several young ladies; the acne improved immediately, however, when they stopped taking the kelp tablets.

Kelp charcoal: For her goiter patients, Ingeborg baked "goiter bread" from knotted wrack *(Ascophyllum nodosum)* meal. She also roasted other brown seaweeds along with knotted wrack until she obtained their ashes (called kelp charcoal) and gave a pinch of this for goiter. Patients who took a pinch or two daily usually seemed to improve more readily.

Pain-freer dilation of body orifices: Tangle *(Laminaria)* stems were occasionally cleaned with an antiseptic and inserted as dilators of body orifices by the physician with whom Ingeborg worked. Because they readily absorb and hold moisture, these naturally swelling dilators provided more pain-free stretching of contracted passages than some of the up-to-date "cold steel" instruments used by modern surgeons. If your physician has to dilate one of your body's openings, say a urethra because of a stricture, you might ask him or her to try leaving a tangle stem in place a while for a possibly less painful dilation.

HOW A SHIP'S PHYSICIAN USED SEAWEED
TO ALLEVIATE HIS URINARY PROBLEM

Sargassum is part of the floating mass of seaweed — the Sargasso Sea — that used to catch and hold sailing ships when the wind died down. Dr. P., doctor on board a cruise ship, found many passengers who, like Dr. P. himself, suffered from stones, kidney troubles and fevers usually associated with urinary ailments. He therefore made a hobby of testing and then prescribing sargassum seaweed salad, soups and teas not only for himself but also for these passengers. They obtained complete relief in a day or so.

His patients enjoyed the relief afforded by this new (for them) way of keeping well so much that many of them continued to use sargassum long after their voyage was over. Dr. P.'s former patients often came back for more cruises and courses of sargassum seaweed treatment, or else they vacationed somewhere along a coast where sargassum washed ashore.

The seaweeds available for sale (at health food stores, gourmet grocers and pharmacies that carry natural health products) are dried, but can certainly be used both in foods and as remedies. The dried products are frequently as effective as the fresh articles.

11

Enhancing Sea Foods with the Curative and Preventive Powers of Lemon, Lime, Garlic, Onion and Olive Oil

The health-bolstering value packed into your sea meals is increased many-fold by the everyday kitchen magic you use in preparing sea foods. Your kitchen magic, of course, includes lemon and lime, garlic, onion, and olive oil. Your kitchen spices, too, have time-honored virtues.

TEN WAYS THAT LEMON ALLEVIATES PAIN AND DISCOMFORT

Because lemon juice is used so often to strike a contrasty note of tartness to the delicate flavor of fish and molluscs, the successful experiences of many people with lemon are given below to guide you in obtaining the fullest value possible from this vitamin-C-rich fruit. Use only fresh, newly cut lemons, not concentrated lemon juice and not so-called lemon juice in plastic lemons.

1. *Lemon and hot bath for edema* — Sady Z. was able to materially reduce her body edema, or dropsy, by taking a hot bath while drinking hot lemonade. She perspired freely and increased her urinary output. Two baths, each followed by a glass of hot lemonade, during the course of a day usually sufficed to relieve her edema. See Chapter 13 for a caution concerning overly hot baths for persons with certain conditions.

2. *Lemon to alleviate corns* — Claude De L. relieved his hard corns by bandaging a slice of lemon over them, or wedging the lemon slice against the soft corns between his toes. Several days of this treatment sufficed to allay his discomfort.

3. *Lemon to relieve itch* — Robert V., a traveling salesman, obtained immediate relief from his scrotal and anal itching by daubing the affected areas with fresh lemon juice.

4. *Lemon, flaxseed and honey for colds* — Julian M., a rural upstate New York pharmacist, relied on a syrup he mixed with two ounces of whole flaxseed, the juice of one lemon, and a tablespoon of warm honey in a pint of boiling water for relieving the miseries of colds, sore throats and hoarseness. He took several sips of the mixture whenever he needed immediate relief. Undiluted lemon juice gargles and mouthwashes, too, helped him to allay the discomfort of sore throat and painful mouth conditions.

5. *Effervescing lemonade to relieve the flu, nausea and headache* — Myra S. ran a tight household and usually caught her children's bouts of flu and grippe in the nick of time with lemon and baking soda. She squeezed a whole lemon into a quarter of a glass of water, and then mixed that with another glass one-quarter filled with water containing one teaspoon of baking soda (or bicarbonate of soda). This resulted in half a glass of vigorously effervescing lemonade. Each of her four children drank half a glass several times a day, starting on the day of the first symptoms. Myra claimed that without this lemonade preventive, the flu attacks would have been much worse. Also, the drink alleviated nausea and vomiting as well as the headachy feeling that often accompanies the flu. Lemon juice in the everyday diet, by the way, has proven to be of some use in reducing the severity of migraine headache.

6. *How to make lemon syrup for colds and nausea* — Lemon syrup can be stored in a well-stoppered, amber-tinted bottle, and added to hot tea or hot water for fighting colds, hoarseness, sore throats, to alleviate nausea, or for a flavorsome drink.

Boil a pint of natural lemon juice for ten minutes, strain through a wad of cotton in a tea strainer, and dissolve two pounds of sugar in it. When the lemon syrup cools, mix in two ounces of almost any distilled beverage or medicinal (ethyl) alcohol.

7. *Lemon and wine for sore throat* — The juice of a lemon in a glass of wine, sometimes chilled with ice, immediately soothed every sore throat that plagued Paul E., a traffic policeman in a large city. Paul drank the lemon and wine only when he was off duty, of course.

8. *Lemons arrest hemorrhage* — One or two swallows of ice-cold lemonade help stop the loss of blood from internal bleeding according to John T., a Florida citrus grower.

9. *Lemon with mineral water relieves asthma* — "Too many drugs on the market for me," Arthur D. complained, "so I use my own remedy for asthma." And he used it with excellent results, he claimed, by taking one or two tablespoonsfuls of fresh lemon juice in a glass of mineral water three times a day.

10. *Lemon relieves rheumatism and gout* — Dr. M., a metropolitan physician who often prescribed fruit for his patients, particularly recommended one or two ounces of freshly squeezed lemon juice in a glass of water three or four times daily for lowering the pulse rate and lessening the severity of attacks of rheumatism and gout.

Too much lemon juice too often, Dr. M. cautioned, could cause some stomach distress or the runs. In such cases, a tablespoon of undiluted lemon juice four times a day sometimes gave better results.

HOW A HOUSEWIFE USED LEMON FOR SKIN CARE

A healthily tanned skin is usually quite welcome. Lucy B., however, for personal reasons, desired to lighten her skin. Before bed, she massaged her face and forehead with a freshly cut lemon and let it dry overnight. In the morning she rinsed her face with a good quality non-perfumed soap and warm water. Within several days, she claimed, the tan left her face, and that was faster than it would have taken without the lemon treatment.

HOW A RESTAURANTEUR OVERCAME
MANY KINDS OF GASTROINTESTINAL DISTRESS

Louis R., a restauranteur in a large southern city, successfully used fresh lemon not only for the flavorful preparation of his famous cuisine, but also to keep his gastrointestinal tract functioning well year after year. Lemon juice, he asserted, is good to drink as follows:

1. As an antidote after an overdose of narcotics has been removed by vomiting (induced by soapy dishwater, extra-strong tea, etc.) or after an alkali poison has been swallowed.

2. To relieve biliousness. Louis R. used one or two ounces of lemon juice with one or two ounces of hot or cold water three or four times a day to remove the offending bile.

3. To stimulate digestion.

4. To alleviate nausea. Mix with baking soda as explained earlier in this section.

5. To relieve jaundice caused by congestion of the liver. Take one or two tablespoonfuls of lemon juice several times a day.

Louis R. also used limes for relieving slight stomach cramps and for promoting good digestion. A very few people might get a temporary skin rash or discoloration from key limes, he believed, although he was not certain whether or not that might be due to some insecticide spray used on the plants. In any case, he used key lime juice to tenderize meat before he cooked it.

Papaya, too, can be used to tenderize meat. The milky juice from the unripe papaya contains an enzyme which, when rubbed onto a tough steak, breaks up the fibers and makes it easier to chew. Be careful, however, not to get this unripe juice into your eyes. In Hawaii, by the way, swimmers use a poultice of pounded papaya leaves to alleviate painful cuts from sharp coral.

A SEA FOOD COCKTAIL THAT LENDS RESISTANCE AGAINST INFECTION, PROMOTES DIGESTION AND STIMULATES GLANDULAR AND KIDNEY FUNCTION

In Central and South America, *seviche* packs a lot of healthy nutrition into a small bowl. *Seviche* is raw flakes of corvina (a Pacific drum) or other non-fatty fish marinated in sour-orange juice (or lime juice as a substitute), cayenne pepper, garlic, onion plus green or red pepper strips. I often enjoyed *seviche* at an open-air restaurant within sight of the Panama Canal...and quickly overlooked the smarting after-taste of the cayenne pepper when I realized what the citrus juice, pepper, garlic, onion, and raw ocean fish meant for my, or anyone's, total health: resistance to infection, stimulation of digestion, and stimulation of glandular and kidney function. Cayenne pepper has also been called a good fat-digester. (When you make *seviche* at home, make certain that the citrus juice covers the fish flakes; marinate three to five hours at room temperature, or overnight in the refrigerator.) Details on *seviche* preparation are given in the section on pickling in Chapter 8.

A SEA FOOD APPETIZER
THAT FIGHTS AGING AND BLOOD CLOTS

Minced fish cooked in vinegar brine with cucumbers, onions and garlic is a traditional food in parts of Europe. The *garlic* and *onion* take the limelight here, not the fish. Garlic has been used as a preventive of atherosclerosis, high blood pressure, gastrointestinal upsets, bronchitis, premature aging and impotence, and many more conditions certainly countered by the enzymes, vitamins and other virtues of garlic. In Germany, they used to say "An onion a day keeps the doctor at bay" *(Ein Zwiebel am Täg halt den Doktor im Schach,* literally, "an onion a day keeps the doctor in check"). And the benefits of the onion have been recognized by a team of physicians at England's Newcastle University (Department of Medicine), where it was found that onions increase the blood's ability to dissolve away dangerous blood clots. Merely a scientific verification of an age-old way of preserving health on an everyday basis!

DAILY GARLIC FOR TWENTY-TWO REASONS

Garlic, another vital plant used in the preparation of sea foods such as bouillabaisse, is literally a lifesaver. When using garlic, start with whole garlic buds, not garlic salts or other prepared garlics. Garlic can be applied directly, raw, to affected areas of your skin or can be eaten as part of a meal. As a snack, it is delicious scraped over hot buttered toast. Also, garlic can be drunk as a tea or syrup.

At an elbow-polished oaken table in the back of a village *Gasthaus* a good three hours walk from any sizeable German town, Simon Z., the sexton, and Hans-Joachim D., the apothecary, sat with me and talked about the virtues of garlic. They knew from their years of experience with self-reliance that daily garlic (in food, as a syrup, or applied as a poultice):

1. Increases appetite and combats skininess.
2. Promotes digestion.
3. Helps expel intestinal parasites. (Worms and insects avoid garlic patches!)
4. Lessens pain in the lower part of the abdomen.
5. Reduces enlarged spleen.
6. Protects against jaundice.
7. Eases hemorrhoidal discomfort. (Apply locally, as well as include it in the diet.)
8. Relieves toothache. (Apply locally.)
9. Alleviates discomfort of gum disease.
10. Relieves coughs.
11. Loosens phlegm in bronchitis.
12. Reduces severity of rheumatic attacks.
13. Discourages development of certain forms of cancer.
14. Retards atherosclerosis.
15. Lowers high blood pressure. (Slows the heart rate and reduces muscle contractility.)
16. Reduces edema or dropsy.
17. Promotes perspiration.
18. Promotes menstrual flow.
19. Promotes labor. (Crush the garlic in milk and drink warm.)
20. Protects against premature aging.
21. Protects against the discomforts of aging.
22. Protects against impotence.

Garlic can have an almost immediate effect, such as increasing the appetite or alleviating toothaches, but most of the above effects of garlic are long-term maintenance benefits obtained by including garlic in the daily diet.

HOW TO PREPARE A WINTER'S SUPPLY
OF GARLIC SYRUP TO FIGHT COUGHS

Her grandfather kept Claire M. and her children supplied with garlic syrup all winter long with this recipe: Chop up and bruise (by pounding) six ounces of fresh garlic. Mix into a pint of vinegar and two pounds of sugar. Let stand four days in a glass container. Filter out any floating matter and then bottle. Claire controlled coughs in her children out on the farm by giving them five to ten drops of this syrup two or three times a day, or even more often if needed.

HOW A GARDENER USED GARLIC FOR SKIN CARE

Lauren G., an avid gardener, sometimes dabbled in more pesticides and chemical agents than his skin could handle, resulting in rashes and irritations on his arms and legs. Too much exposure to certain plants, too, occasionally caused him severe itching. He was fairly successful in alleviating much of this discomfort overnight by applying a mixture of crushed garlic, salt and olive oil to the affected spots. Lauren G. also claimed that garlic mashed with honey lightened the brown "liver" spots that appeared from time to time on his arms.

TWELVE WAYS THAT ONION FIGHTS ACHES AND DISEASES, AND REGULATES UNBALANCED BODY FUNCTIONS

Onion not only helps you to create magnificent sea food platters, but has been praised, just as garlic has been, by hundreds of people from all walks of life who have had successful experiences with onion. And much of this experience has been scientifically documented.

An Appalachian school teacher and her Austrian horticulturist husband, gave the following uses of onion according to their own successful results for immediate relief, or for cumulative long-term benefits over the years:

1. Regulation of gastrointestinal function, stimulation of secretion and better appetite.
2. Relief of constipation (cooked onions, especially in sauces, are helpful).
3. Promotion of urinary flow.
4. Flushing out of kidney gravel or grit. (Onion, however, could further irritate your kidneys if you already have some kinds of kidney inflammation or infection.)
5. Control of anemia.
6. Relief of earache. Mix two teaspoonfuls of fresh onion juice plus two teaspoonfuls of olive oil, then put four to six warmed drops in the affected ear; repeat if needed in half an hour.
7. Lessening of high blood pressure.
8. Relief and healing of minor burns. Crush fresh onion and apply directly.

9. Lubrication of dry mucous membranes.
10. Soothing hoarseness.
11. Relief of bronchitis. Take a teaspoon of freshly squeezed onion juice and sugar; a teaspoon every three to four hours.
12. Relief of pneumonia. Mix up a poultice of boiled onion, flaxseed meal and vinegar, then pack it on the chest and in the armpits. (I specifically asked whether it was pneumonia itself or only pneumonia-*like* chest conditions that responded well to the onion poultice. The teacher and her husband insisted that it was actual pneumonia.)

In all of the above uses, even the ones for which specific uses of onion are given for immediate effects, you can achieve good long-term effects by a diet that regularly includes onion...eaten raw or cooked, drunk in teas or syrups, or cooked in soups and gravies.

THE DISINFECTANT POWERS OF RAW ONION

Because daily use of onions during the winter builds resistance to colds, sore throats and infections, and because onions retard the growth of some disease organisms, Gertrude Y., the bookkeeper-wife of the director of a private clinical laboratory that specialized in doing microbiological tests for physicians in the downtown area of a large city, convinced several of these physicians to try her onion-slice disinfection system. Her simple and rather primitive "devices" consisted of large slices of raw onion placed at several places in a sickroom. She contended (and apparently was backed up by the bacterial cultures she made from dust in different areas of the rooms) that her system helped control air-borne dust and other particles laden with disease-causing organisms from patients suffering with pneumonia and other contagious diseases, and thereby helped to control the spread of disease.

HOW ONIONS ALLEVIATE
COUGHS AND THROAT IRRITATIONS

Onion and sugar for convulsive coughing: Sara F. used her instant cough reliever whenever her children or her aged father had a coughing spell during the winter. She liberally sprinkled granulated sugar over a large, freshly cut slice of raw onion. A teaspoonful of the resulting thick syrup every fifteen to twenty minutes soothed coughs almost at once.

Onion and almond milk for hefty coughing and throat irritation:
Onion juice squeezed fresh into almond "milk" (almond oil dispersed in water) makes a soothing cough mixture that can be used by the teaspoonful every half hour or so for violent coughing, according to Captain Tom, a Mississippi tugboat operator. Relief is usually after a dose or two.

Captain Tom relied on the soothing, protective powers of almond oil almost as much as he relied on onion juice. A few words on almonds, therefore, might be of interest, as well as of practical use. Almonds have been known since biblical times. Sweet almonds (the domesticated trees) or bitter almonds (usually the wild trees) are sometimes used interchangeably...with proper precautions (tiny doses, that is, a few drops) taken because of the possible poisonous content of some *bitter* almond kernels. Oil of *sweet* almond is probably safer for cooking and internal use. A few drops of almond oil soothe congestion and irritated mucous membranes of the digestive system or chest, and help relieve convulsive coughing, bronchitis and asthmatic bouts.

Almond oil rubbed into the skin, too, soothes and refreshes, especially when discomfort is caused by pressure sores that form on persons who lean constantly on one spot (such as persons confined to wheelchairs or beds). A massage with almond oil revitalizes tired and aching feet caused by standing for long periods of time.

Outdoorsmen and people who are constantly exposed to the weather and to humidity, like Captain Tom, use almond oil to protect their skin from the rigors of long exposure to excess moisture, dryness, heat or cold. Actors rub almond oil on their faces to counter the irritation of continually loading their faces with makeup. Almond oil dispersed in water (almond "milk" emulsion) is a substitute for mother's milk for infants who cannot obtain or cannot tolerate real milk. Almond oil and extracts are available in gourmet food stores as well as in some pharmacies and health food shops.

How to make almond milk: If you choose to start with almonds themselves, and not the oil, put a handful (a third of a cup) of shelled almonds in a collander or sieve and immerse a moment in boiling water; then leave them near (but not directly on) the burner awhile, until you can slip off the brownish skins from the nut kernels. Cool the skinned almonds in iced water for several minutes. (This *blanching* with boiling water followed by quick cooling stops enzymatic action, especially that which is responsible for loss of some vitamins.) Using a mortar and pestle, pound, to a smooth paste, the skinned almonds plus two tablespoonfuls of sugar and five tablespoonfuls of water (preferably distilled or bottled water). Squeeze the almond paste through a fine strainer. Use the paste as is, or dilute with water by vigorously shaking the paste with a cupful of water in a shaker or screw-top jar until you have an emulsion of the almond oil suspended in the water — your almond "milk."

OLIVES — FAMOUS FOR THOUSANDS OF YEARS OF HEALTH

I brought a jar of glistening, greenish-black Greek olives and nibbled on these slightly fermented fruits of the gods while I waited in a barber shop for a haircut. "You got the secret of life right there in that jar young man," Stavros P., the proprietor, said as he beamed at me over the head of a client in the chair. Stavros enumerated the benefits of olives, and particularly of olive oil, in his and his family's daily diet. Olives and their oil:

1. Relieve gallbladder disorders, especially gallstones.
2. Act as a gentle laxative, especially for expectant mothers or people with hemorrhoids.
3. Help reduce frequency and severity of chronic colds.
4. Soften crusty scabs that form during head colds. (Use a few drops on the scabs.)
5. Alleviate rheumatic pains. (Massage into skin.)
6. Help expel worms from the intestinal tract.
7. Soothe chapped skin. (Rub in well after a warm bath. If, however, this tends to tan your skin too much, then expose the oil to the sun to bleach it a bit before use.)
8. Tone up the heart.
9. Stimulate hair growth. (Massage into the scalp regularly.)

The man in Stavros's barber chair was nodding in accord with what Stavros was saying; so much so, in fact, that the Greek barber had to move his straight razor away so as not to cut his client's ear. "All that makes sense to me medically," the man in the chair said, "except maybe the part about growing hair; although I've heard from old-timers that regular massaging of the scalp seems to help some people to grow it. One or two of my patients get a little bilious when they take too much olive oil, so I usually don't recommend their taking more than two or three tablespoons a day. On the other hand, my patients tolerate much more, especially when they take the oil with meals that include acid fruit, like pineapples, lemons and apples." Then Dr. G., the man in Stavros' barber chair, reached out and helped himself to the last olives in my jar.

12

Healing and Rejuvenation Powers of Sea, Sand and Sun

HOW SEACOAST CLIMATE
SUSTAINS HEALTH AND ALLEVIATES DISEASE

Seacoast climate is characterized by more frequent yet milder changes in the weather and temperature than occur further inland — air in motion (especially the invigorating land and sea breezes), pulsing surf, solar radiation, sand, and atmosphere rich in natural aerosole (that is, vaporized sea spray). Seacoast air may contain as much as thirty times more iodine than the air further inland. The low pH (indicating an acid rather than an alkaline state) of seacoast breezes probably weakens air-borne, disease-causing microorganisms, making them more liable to be overcome by your body's own defenses. Physiologically, marine climate intensifies the protective action of the body's cells and fluids against disease.

When you arrive at the sea for the season's first swim, your metabolism sharply increases in response to the seawater, its wave surge, the atmosphere and the sunshine. The changes in your body over the first three to ten days at the coast may be so brusque that you might rightly wonder whether you are getting better or getting worse than you were upon arrival. You are probably getting better.

157

However, a stay at seaside areas with a vigorous climate may be somewhat too much all at once for you if you have a thyroid condition, insomnia, a tendency to continuously suffer new bouts of rheumatism (although rheumatism is sometimes alleviated during the summer months at the sea), coronary sclerosis, some gastrointestinal disorders, certain kidney problems, or certain gynecological disorders. Some vacationers who are sensitive to noise and movement may not feel in top shape at the beach, where air and sea are constantly shifting to the tune of whooshing, whistling or groaning winds. Others, however, even if they are sensitive to changes in the weather, usually find alleviation of many conditions if they are not inconvenienced by the movement and sound that are part-and-parcel of the real charm (charm in the sense of a real magical spell!) and curative power of the sea.

A stay at the sea is excellent for colds and upper respiratory tract infections. Colds are associated with civilization and a general softening or loss of hardiness. Our tendency to catch cold is in part due to easy-going civilized ways, sedentary city life and the loss of our natural reactivity to extreme temperatures. The overheated and excessively blood-congested mucosal surfaces of the nose, mouth and the rest of the upper respiratory passages have lost much of their capacity to deal with drops in environmental temperature. Ultrasonically atomized seawater is a standard treatment at some marinotherapeutic centers, as shown in the photograph below.

In a few cases, the changeover from city to seashore may be so radical for the system that a person who lives temporarily in the clean air at the coast may be particularly susceptible to infection when he returns to his city. Usually, however, the resistance built up during a stay at the seaside carries over and helps protect us for some time after the visit. Like any other vacation or change of usual pace, the seaside vacation catches us in time to dissipate accumulating stress and other ills that undermine our resistance to disease and ill health.

A stay at the seaside — in its atmosphere, water and surf, and sand — provides a vital second breath, a chance to let the systems of your body get back into shape — to recharge, so to speak, your batteries after serious illness, loss of blood, excessively severe physical or mental exhaustion or stress.

Iodine is one of the sea's gifts of health to us. Some of the benefits of iodine are obtainable by merely breathing at seacoasts which

Courtesy of German Information Center

These three spa guests are relieving chronic respiratory conditions by inhaling ultrasonically atomized seawater at Westerland auf Sylt, a North Sea marinotherapeutic resort. The white, hooded gowns are worn to protect clothing from the room's salty atmosphere.

Fig. 11

are rich in seaweeds, and by bathing in mineral-rich seawater, although some coastal waters are richer than others in iodine and other minerals. Iodine helps build resistance to rheumatism, alleviates menstrual and menopausal disorders, and absorbs severe bleeding that certain conditions occasion in the thick fluid of the eyeball. The healthy thyroid gland needs iodine to carry out its normal functions; goiter, a thyroid condition, can occur when there is a lack of iodine, and, in fact, there are iodine-poor areas in the world where goiter is somewhat of a traditional disease that everyone accepts as part of the local environment. In Bavaria, for example, the size of a young lady's swollen neck — a sign of goiter — has been used to measure her beauty...the more swollen her neck, the greater her beauty in the eyes of the local lads! Drinking or bathing in water containing iodine has been successful in overcoming female sterility and protecting expectant mothers against premature birth of their children.

The seacoast and tuberculosis: There does not seem to be one perfect climate that is ideal for combating tuberculosis; however, this disease does heal better in climates that are suitable, on an *individual* basis, for a particular person's tuberculosis. That is, when you do find what seems to alleviate your own case of the disease, then it is probably good in your case, regardless of what it does for others. Sea climate, even in winter, is usually good for persons whose tuberculosis does not involve the lungs (but is not usually good for pulmonary tuberculosis, especially in children). Sea bathing is a good preventive for young people threatened by tuberculosis, that is, children who, perhaps because of constitutional weaknesses, are especially prone to the effects of poor nutrition, congested and unclean living spaces, association with tubercular persons, undue and unrelenting stress, and other conditions that tear down natural resistance.

The seacoast and obesity: A cool seacoast is good for you if you are obese and wish to reduce, but watch out for beefed-up appetites! Hot sand baths or salt thermal baths, on the other hand, step up your body's burning of food without increasing your appetite. Persons with high blood pressure or atherosclerosis should not take very hot baths; persons whose nerves easily fatigue should not take very cold baths.

Obese persons will find it useful to know that drinks of cold water increase oxidation (or burning up) of nutrients, and that sulfate-containing mineral water reduces the body's use of food and increases metabolism. Too much sulfate might act as an abortifacient, and is therefore not recommended for pregnant women. After delivery, and during the weaning period, however, sulfate-containing mineral water may be used.

Persons who are both obese and prone to gallstone problems should avoid frequent, inconsistent dieting that causes repeated ups and downs in weight; this could increase the risk of developing gallstones, according to studies supported by the National Institute of Arthritis, Metabolic and Digestive Diseases.

Seaside effect on eczema: Eleven-year old Katy's chronic eczema cleared up after a month and a half at the sea. Her mother said it took only a week to clear up during vacation the year before. One of Katy's cousins who had a similar eczema took two months to show any improvement.

Psoriasis treatment at the Dead Sea: One of the saltiest of seas is the Dead Sea — 1,286 feet below (normal) sea level. People suffering from psoriasis are treated there for four weeks with four to six hours of sunbathing every day, interspersed with several twenty-minute bathing spells in the Dead Sea, petrolatum jelly applications to the skin and plenty of rest and relaxation. Sunburn, by the way, is less severe at the Dead Sea than at resorts at higher elevations because of less reddening radiation from the sun at the level of the Dead Sea.

Effect of seacoast air on bronchial asthma and other allergic conditions: The clean, penetrating air of the sea is free of pollen and industrial pollution. Some port areas, however, do discharge contaminants into the air. Seacoast forests can produce pollen, too, that might disturb some allergic persons. If you suffer from asthma, it is usually better for you to keep to the open beach and to avoid mudflats or stagnating areas behind the beach where molds or other substances might disturb you if you have any allergies that make you sensitive to them.

Pollen-free sea air...and pollen bread for resistance to colds and relief of prostatitis: During my discussions with staff members of a seaside resort about the pollen-free sea climate and how that benefits persons with certain allergies, Lars B., a Scandinavian ski instructor (who was at the resort to recuperate from skiing injuries and subsequent surgery), insisted that he included pollen in the diet of the atheletes he trained! This claim intrigued me (perhaps because I once spent a full academic year analyzing fresh pollen, drilling for prehistoric pollen grains from the bottom of lakes in New York State, and memorizing the details of hundreds of kinds of pollen grains under a microscope!), so I checked around further until I found out that the Swedes had an allergy-free pollen extract that increased resistance to respiratory tract infections, helped relieve certain kinds of prostatitis, and permitted some diabetics to reduce their insulin dosage.

Dr. E., an Atlanta physician attending a seminar at the seaside resort, suggested that eating large amounts of whole pollen as food might provide some of these benefits. This could be done with cattails (*Typha* species), a common waterside plant found growing in marshes, ponds and along canal banks. The bright, golden yellow pollen grains, rich in Vitamin A, that cover the topmost flowering spikes of cattails can be used with or in place of ordinary flour to bake biscuits or pancakes, or steamed to make cattail pollen bread. (Young cattail shoots can be boiled like asparagus; and young

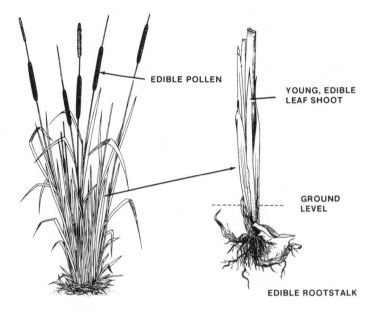

EDIBLE POLLEN

YOUNG, EDIBLE
LEAF SHOOT

GROUND
LEVEL

EDIBLE ROOTSTALK

Fig. 12

spikes, before the pollen grains appear, can be boiled or steamed for tasty eating.) Dr. E. ate cattail pollen muffins only for gourmet reasons, because he thought that the heat used in baking the pollen meal might lessen its medicinal value. For medicinal purposes (he had prostatitis), Dr. E. took a commercially prepared pollen extract from Sweden. That Swedish extract was combined with a sea product (fish liver oil) in a tablet called Cernelle, which also contains all the known vitamins (except B_{12}), twenty-one amino acids, peptides, enzymes, coenzymes, calcium, iron, silicon, potassium, copper, magnesium, manganese, zinc, titanium, molybdenum, sulfur, phosphorus, chlorine, boron, cobalt, brewer's yeast, rose hips, sterines and other biofactors.

The Swedes also combine pollen extract with powdered seaweed from the Arctic Ocean in *Beltux capsules,* which also contain vitamins (A, B_1, B_2, calcium pantothenate, niacin, B_6, folic acid, B_{12}, C, choline, inositol, K, rutin, E), amino acids, nucleic acid components, calcium phosphate, plus iodine and the minerals listed above for Cernelle tablets. Cernelle, Beltux and other preparations that include Arctic seaweed are made by the Cernelle Company, Vegelholm 6250, Engelholm, Sweden. In Sweden, by the way, pollinating insects are protected by legislation against herbicides and insecticides, so the pollen used for the above tablets and capsules is collected from fields that are free of dangerous chemicals.

The effect of sunlight on skin conditions: In his southeastern seaboard medical practice, Dr. S. found that ichthyosis ("fishskin" or scaly skin disease) and psoriasis responded well to treatment that included sunlight, and this was therefore his standard treatment for these conditions. Sunlight generally helped control ordinary acne (acne vulgaris) and seborrheic eczema (in which the oil or sebaceous glands secrete excessive amounts of oil), but not highly inflamed acute eczema. Sunlight also helped alleviate pityriasis (branny scales), pruritis that occurs in the very elderly or in diabetics, pyoderma (inflammatory conditions with pus), leg ulcers, and some kinds of trichophytosis (fungus infection of skin, hair, nails). Dr. S. also found that sunbathing helped to clear up poorly healing wounds.

Dr. S. called to my attention a recent development by some of his colleagues in Tennessee, whose work with caffeine in the treatment of eczema is described below, and will be of interest to you if eczema troubles you.

Caffeine cures eczema: More than one physician has described the overusage of "modern miracle drugs" and sought out the naturally occurring substances and forces (like Dr. S. has done with sunlight) that surround us every day... like coffee and tea. Dermatologists at the University of Tennessee School of Medicine came up with an ointment made from caffeine, a mild stimulant that occurs naturally in coffee and tea, which improved fifteen of seventeen patients suffering from eczema; the ointment was applied for three weeks. Unlike the steroid creams sometimes used for skin conditions, the caffeine ointment had no side effects.

It is not so strange that these dermatologists came up with a cure from the kitchen, so to speak. Traditionally, dermatologists have been the backroom dabblers in chemistry and pharmacy... and justifiably so, for skin diseases have been among the toughest of diseases to cure, and the hardest of them for us to understand biologically, psychologically and chemically. (Note that I write *cure* before *understand* — cures are quite possible even before complex causes comes to light, fortunately for us.)

In general, caffeine (from the dried leaves of Chinese or other tea, dried coffee beans, African kola nuts, and other plants) stimulates the nervous system and heart, promotes urinary flow and alleviates nervous headache. Coffee has a long reputation of being good for chronic asthma. For this purpose, it must be newly roasted, not burned too much, and drunk strong, soon after grinding.

Effect of sun, warmth, and cold on diabetics: Coldness is generally unfavorable for diabetics, although cold seawater baths increase sugar in the blood without causing glycosuria (sugar in the urine), which is of interest to diabetics because one of their constant concerns is to keep down the sugar in their urine. Generally, mildly warm water is more favorable than cold for diabetics.

Too much sunbathing can cause a sharp drop in the amount of sugar in the blood, leading to insulin shock in some diabetics.

Long seaside vacations tend to increase the normal body's tolerance of glucose because of its improved production in the liver and stepped-up oxidation, or burning, in the tissues; the diabetic, however, cannot always burn up his sugar. So, although the seacoast is good for quite a few mildly diabetic persons, seriously diabetic persons may not fare as well there.

HOW SEAWATER AND MINERAL WATERS
SUSTAIN HEALTH AND ALLEVIATE DISEASE

Seawater is of vital interest to our health not only because it gives rise to all of the animal and plant life that bring us food and health, but also because it is itself capable of healing and preserving health. Ocean voyages, boating along shore, fishing and beach-combing, of course, all help us to expose ourselves to the healing and rejuvenating powers of the sea. Swimming and wading, however, bring our bodies into intimate contact with the sea's pulsating wave action, minerals and dissolved gases.

Bathing in the sea acts directly on specific diseases and disorders and indirectly on the whole organism, helping to overcome chronic or long-lasting conditions, and tranquilizing the whole nervous system.

Bathing in cool seawater calms down overwrought nerves, yet also tones up the system so as to keep it resilient enough to effectively handle stressful situations and thereby prevent becoming more overwrought — it breaks a vicious circle.

Bathing in warm seawater, that is, about body temperature, improves circulation in the arms and legs, and helps muscles to contract healthfully, thus putting the body in good shape for exercise.

Sea bathing makes a significant contribution to your rehabilitation and toughening-up if you are convalescing from an illness. Young children, the very elderly, and weakened persons, however, should take care not to expose themselves to very cold water too abruptly. However, short, cool wading baths in the ocean, for elderly people whose health can tolerate them, tone up the heart and circulation.

The effect on us of *iodine* in the seawater was described in an earlier section. *Potassium* in the seawater in which we bathe enters the skin encourages good urinary flow and increases the effect of the vitamins we get from our food. *Magnesium* has an anti-allergic effect on skin and bronchioles (thus helping control bronchial asthma), as well as a sedative and spasm-relieving effect. *Bromine* tranquilizes the nervous system. (The magnesium concentration in the Dead Sea is about 15 times greater, and the bromine concentration about 50 times greater, than in ocean water.) *Calcium* has an anti-inflammatory effect and also helps combat allergies. Don't doubt that the sea is full of the bone-building material calcium, for that is just where all of the shell-carrying animals get it, and where the tiny coral polyps get it to build their huge coral reefs! Inhalation of salt vapors (sodium and chloride) stimulates the whole body, and promotes the removal of unhealthy secretions and phlegm (see photograph earlier in this chapter, which shows how ultrasonically atomized seawater is used at a marinotherapeutic center in Germany). A drink of salt water (a cup or so every few hours, depending upon how salty it is, your diet, etc.) is a powerful regulator that normalizes your stomach acidity. If your stomach juices are too acid salt water reduces the acidity. If, on the other hand, your stomach juices are not acid enough, salt water increases the acidity. That is one of the marks of a good natural curative substance: it *normalizes* body function and acts to protect you from extremes.

In general, seawater drinks have been recommended warm or cold, plain or mixed (with freshwater, carbonated water, cognac, lemon juice or lime juice). A four-week drinking schedule that has been used with good results is explained below:

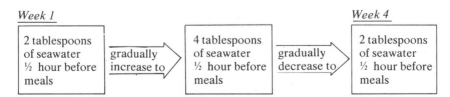

Week 1

| 2 tablespoons of seawater ½ hour before meals | gradually increase to | 4 tablespoons of seawater ½ hour before meals | gradually decrease to | 2 tablespoons of seawater ½ hour before meals |

Week 4

A British farmer told me how a daily glassful of a few table-spoons of seawater, rainwater, some vinegar and honey alleviated his rheumatism and his sore throat.

Tides and currents: When you deal with the ocean as a power-ful friend, however, take care to realize that anything powerful also has its hazardous aspects. The sea, a powerful medicine, has its tides and currents, which may offer some risk in some places at some times. Always check with local people about how the tides and currents behave along their part of the coast. Occasional amateur (and even some professional) biologists and beachcombers, who were out collecting sea animals and seaweeds, have been sorely surprised far out on mudflats or dry sandbars by a suddenly return-ing tide that flooded upon them and suddenly cut them off from the mainland. Luckily, in the cases I know about, the biologists were dragging along small, beach-style air mattresses behind them on to which they tossed the sponges, seaweeds, sea urchins and marine snails they were collecting. So, when the water started to slosh in around their ankles, they quickly paddled back to shore. Resorts and other inhabited coastal areas, however, are usually free of such hazards, or else erect clear warning signals at any spot where cau-tion should be exercised at certain times of the day or year.

Effect of seawater and mineral waters on gout and kidney gravel: A few sips (at regular intervals) of seawater over the course of a stay at a seaside resort, and according to the recommendations of spa personnel who know the particular strength of their local water, promote the excretion of uric acid, thus removing some of the cause of the uric acid crystals that are involved in the pain and discomfort of gout and some kinds of urinary tract gravel. Mineral waters from alkaline and salt springs, too, often act like seawater in relieving these conditions.

Salted mineral water loosens constipation: During his spa stay, Clyde S. learned to relieve his constipation by drinking a glass of salted mineral water (various kinds worked) before breakfast. The *Bademeister* (or bath master) at Clyde's spa had long since resolved his own constipation problem by drinking salted mineral water; he kept himself open by eating one orange and drinking one glass of cold water every morning before breakfast. (A swallow of any cold water, by the way, can stimulate a bowel movement before the water even reaches the intestines!)

Twelve mineral waters to make you feel better: The window display of a large, established (30 years) liquor store caught my attention...it was all bottles of mineral water! Anton J., the owner, said "Good mineral waters are worth every inch of my valuable window space."

Anton himself and his family drank active mineral water, not plain bottled distilled water that has all of its minerals removed. His interest in mineral waters began when he learned that of the six public sources of tap water and four known brands of U.S. bottled water tested in the Washington, D.C. area, only one (a mineral water from Hot Springs, Arkansas) was completely free of bacteria. So, his interest sparked, he began looking into the other benefits of many kinds of bottled mineral waters. To begin with, daily gargling with any one of many kinds of mineral waters relieved Anton's throat irritation from too much smoking. Also, Anton's store manager was afforded some relief from stomach distress and too much sugar in the blood and urine by daily drinks of *Apollinaris* water, a mineral water from Bad Neuenahr, Germany. This water from the alkaline springs of Bad Neuenahr, by the way, helps discourage formation of uric acid stones. Phosphate and carbonate stones, on the other hand, are discouraged by gypsum or sulfate waters, such as *Vittel* and *Contrexéville* water (both from France). Anton told me that Italian *Fiuggi* water helped his customers who suffered from kidney stones (it is used today in Italy, where it was also a favorite drink of Michelangelo hundreds of years ago. Anton's window also contains other European mineral waters: *Badoit* (from St. Galmier, France), sparkling *Bru* and *Spa Reine* (from Spa, Belgium), *Evian* (from the French Alps), *Perrier* (from Vergeze, France), *San Pellegrino* (from Bergamo, Italy), *Solares* (from Santander, Spain), and *Vichy Celestins* (from Vichy, France). All of these bottled (in *glass,* not plastics or other materials that could lead to contamination) waters are completely free of added chlorine or other chemicals (except the natural minerals that come from the natural springs where the waters are bottled); carbon dioxide is sometimes added during bottling, but it is often the spring's own natural carbon dioxide gas that is merely being piped in separately to avoid loss. Most of these waters are sold in supermarkets, liquor stores or directly by distributors. If you have difficulty finding any of these time-proven European waters, write to Mountain Valley Spring Co., Hot Springs, Arkansas 71909, for the address of local distributors.

HOW SAND AND SEA MUDS
SUSTAIN HEALTH AND ALLEVIATE DISEASE

Sand: Packing warm, dry sand over you, outside in the open sunlight, does wonders for you if you suffer from rheumatic pains. Relatively higher temperatures can be tolerated with this dry (rather than moist) heat. Indoor sand baths, too, can be quite effective in relieving pains and discomfort. The photograph below illustrates sand boxes being used at a German bathhouse. Such a box can be built quite simply from several lengths of lumber. Take care, however, in piling too much sand over your chest, for sand is heavy, and that could impair your breathing movements. So a bathtub is probably not a good container for sand, as that could tempt you to use too much sand.

When walking over light, sandy beaches, be aware that the reflecting ultraviolet radiation from seaside sand can redden and burn

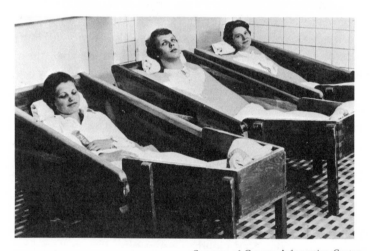

Courtesy of German Information Center

Renate S., a dental technician, has just taken a hot mud bath in 275 pounds of freshly cut peat and 70 quarts of water to alleviate her slipped disc condition. The peat bath penetrated her body with seven times as much heat as plain water would have given her...and that didn't even burn her. Here she is shown as a physiotherapist rinses off the therapeutic peat-mud at Bad Aibling in Upper Bavaria, Germny. Bad Aibling specializes in rheumatic, urinary and nervous system disorders, and women's ailments.

Fig. 13

your untanned legs and feet if you are a newly arrived, unacclimated visitor with cream-cheese white skin.

Sea muds: Sea muds contain organic matter, minerals and may even be radioactive (such as at Igalo, one of Yugoslavia's spas on the Adriatic Sea). North Sea mud, say from around Wilhelmshaven in Germany, is made of silica-containing diatoms (microscopic, one-cell algae), microorganisms that break down sulfates, calcium from once-living organisms, various other organic matter, and clay. Part of the favorable effect of this sea mud on rheumatism, gout, arthritis, neuralgia and various skin conditions is due to the mud's being a poor conductor of heat (thus retaining it), its sulfur content, and the friction (or stimulating counterirritation) caused by the minuscule silica-rich skeletons of the diatoms and other gritty particles in the clay. To prepare the mud for bathing in it, spa personnel heat it up and mix in seawater until it is of a comfortable consistency. Various mud packs that may be similar to some sea muds are available from manufacturers and distributors that supply reputable beauty and skin-care specialists.

Therapeutic, mineral-containing muds for home treatment can be obtained from the ancient Tiberias hot springs (first mentioned as Hammath or Chamat in Joshua 19:35) on the shore of the Sea of Galilee, about eighteen miles from Nazareth. For information, contact the Israeli Government Tourist Office, 488 Madison Avenue, New York, New York 10022. Also, some of the European spas and resorts listed at the end of this chapter can either supply or else tell you where to obtain the muds they use.

Peat mud, too, is quite effective in relieving pain and providing actual curative action, especially in certain female disorders. The photo on page 170 shows Renate S. just as she steps out of 275 pounds of peat mud, in which she bathed to relieve her slipped disc problem. Peat mud contains organic and even hormonal substances, whereas sea mud is more inorganic and mineralized.

HOW TO AVOID THE DISCOMFORT OF SKIN IRRITATIONS AT THE BEACH AND IN THE WATER BIKINI DERMATITIS

Chemical analysis indicated that a dye called Disperse Blue 35, used in some bathing suits, may have been part of the cause of irritation and darkened patches of skin after Lucy R. exposed her body to bright sunlight. After sunbathing and sweating profusely, she felt a burning sensation and noted reddening under the straps of her brown bikini. (Disperse Blue 35 dye is used for brown as well as blue textiles.) Despite her washing the bathing suit before her

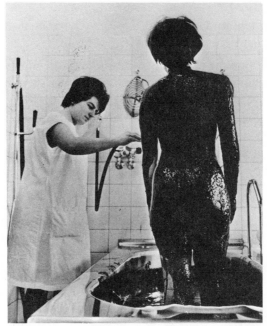

Courtesy of German Information Center

These visitors to the Oeynhausen public bath (in the North Rhein-Westphalia region of Germany) are enjoying the pain-freeing benefits of warm sand baths. Oeynhausen specializes in therapy for guests with cardiovascular, rheumatic and nervous diseases, and women's ailments.

Fig 14

next sunbath, the same irritation occurred. She discarded the bikini, and, several months later, the darkened patches cleared up. Another sunbather, Carol G., developed the same burning and skin darkening, but her suit was dark blue. The dermatologists who studied these two cases were convinced of a connection between the dye or dyes in the bikini suits and the skin problems that occurred in the two women who wore those suits. The point here is to change bathing suits if you have unexplainable skin darkening and burning irritation following sunbathing and sweating. (This is a phototoxic reaction; that is, sunlight causes the dye to affect the skin. Certain plants, too, can cause skin irritation under the effect of light.)

Seabather's eruption or marine dermatitis can bother you if you swim on the Atlantic and Gulf coasts of Florida: sometimes from about March to September, although not predictably every year. It has also been reported in parts of the Caribbean. Your skin will begin to sting *under* your bathing suit, perhaps even before you leave the water. Raised, reddened spots or wheals — like insect bites — will show up during the first day after leaving the water. Although you might experience chills and fever in a severe case of seabather's eruption, the itching most usually subsides without further annoyance in a few days. To allay discomfort, remove your bathing suit and wash it well with soap. If necessary, apply ice or cold compresses to reduce inflammation or swelling. The cause of seabather's eruption is not clearly understood. The cause of swimmer's itch, however, is known and described below.

Swimmer's itch or muck itch often occurs after swimming in freshwater ponds or lakes, such as the lakes of Minnesota, Wisconsin and Michigan, or in those tiny rock-quarry lakes around which homes may be built in suburban "lake" communities. You may feel a prickling sensation and see a rash almost at once but it will clear up in a few weeks. Or, itching might begin as late as a week or so after swimming. Little blister-topped pimples appear. The itching and blisters occur only on the skin that was *uncovered* by the bathing suit. Parts of the body that were protected by a closely fitting bathing suit are not affected. If you wipe off the lake or pond water and shower with soap at once, you may be able to stop the itch by removing the burrowing larvae responsible for the itch and rash. (These are larvae of trematodes or flatworms that parasitize snails and waterfowl in freshwater lakes and ponds, but also find their way accidentally under *our* skin.)

Sea strings or needle-like pteropods may penetrate your bathing suit and skin if you bathe in the Gulf of Mexico and cause wheals in your skin. Wash with soap. Alleviate discomfort with compresses dipped in ice water. Ammonia water flooded over the skin area that stings may help, too.

Portuguese man-of-war strings were alleviated with aloes by Norman L. in this way: he rubbed aloe leaf pulp on the stings for immediate relief from pain as well as to help reduce swelling. Norman also reported that a plaster of the fresh, moist leaf pulp over an abscess draws out the purulent matter; and that a split leaf, or merely sap from the leaf, soothes wounds of many kinds. Pulp has also been rubbed on burns to relieve pain and help prevent scars. Any of several species of aloe have been used as remedies, although the effect may differ according to species or geographical variety of aloe used. Let's take a moment to describe a few other virtues of aloe, as long as we have this chance to talk about such a proven pain-freeing plant!

For a tea to help fight *colds and biliousness,* by the way, Norman's grandmother, who was raised in the Caribbean near the island of Curaçao, boiled a piece of leaf and drank several cups or so of the liquid as needed during the day. She always cautioned her friends, however, to use only small amounts of aloe internally, because heavy internal use could lead to kidney inflammation, slight gastro-enteritis, irritation, or perhaps some cramping.

For a *laxative,* Norman's grandmother scraped out the pulp from a piece of aloe leaf and beat it with one egg, then took a cup or so of this mixture a day to loosen up ordinary constipation.

To lessen the pains of *rheumatism,* or the irritation caused by *insect bites and stings,* a friend of Norman's grandmother rubbed the pellicule (or leaf skin) over the spot closest to the pain or irritation. (The pellicule contains a substance that acts as a counterirritant, often affording a great deal of immediate relief.)

For *diabetes,* a Hawaiian herbalist peeled and scraped about one cupful of leaf pulp, blended it into one gallon of water, then drank one cup of this aloe punch daily for one to four weeks to allay his diabetes. Cortez's soldiers drank aloe sap to cure themselves of scurvy and anemia. There are reports, too, of moist, hot packs made from aloe, pulp and sap being used to treat external signs of *venereal disease* — mainly gonorrhea. Preparations made from the root have been used to treat syphilis.

Drugstores and health foodstores have aloe extract and aloe sunburn ointment.

HOW TO PROTECT SKIN FROM EXCESS SUN, MOISTURE AND DRYNESS

A manufacturing chemist and one-time village apothecary, Luigi D., made a career of developing cosmetics for industry. His own bag of toiletries, however, struck me by its simplicity. (I shared a compartment on an international train with Luigi, so I personally witnessed how he cared for his own face and skin for a whole week of hot summer weather.) Luigi's basic formulas for skin care were not trade secrets, but were well known to the industry, and can be compounded for you by any pharmacist with a well-stocked shop. Here are three of them:

1. *Petroleum jelly for protection from excess sun* can be made of amber petroleum jelly (86 grams), lanolin (6 grams), insoluble brown pigment (5 grams), a sun screen to filter out ultraviolet rays, such as menthyl salicylate (2.5 grams), and floral water or perfume (0.5 grams).

2. *Suntan lotion for acquiring a tan* can be made of a soluble brown pigment (5 parts) mixed with floral water (95 parts).

3. *Soothing sunburn ointment* can be made of cetasal emulsion (95 parts), bornyl salicylate (2.25 parts), carotene oil (2.25 parts), and menthol (0.5 parts). Sunburn can also be alleviated with 20% cetasal emulsion (95 parts), carotene oil (2 parts), halibut oil (2 parts), and lavender oil (1 part).

TWO METHODS
OF SAFELY AND GRADUALLY BENEFITING
FROM THE SUN'S HEALING POWERS

The English navigator Sir Francis Drake, the first captain to personally (without dying en route as Magellan did earlier) take his ship around the globe, sailed through many kinds of climate during that voyage of 1577 to 1580. He was able to feel in himself and observe in his crew the effects of those climates, of which he wrote in his journal:

> ...so that even after our departure from the heate wee alwayes found our bodies not as sponges, but strong and hardened, more able to beare out cold, though wee came out of excesse of heate, than a number of chamber champions could have beene, who lye on their feather-beds till they go to sea, or rather whose teeth in a temperate aire do beate in their heads...by the fire.

Drake thus ridiculed the soft, enfeebling habits of some of his fellow seafarers. We, like Drake's crew, can toughen up and build resistance against diseases by taking energy from the sun. But Drake's crew did it *gradually,* at sailing (not jetliner) speed. The following are several *gradual* ways to take this healing solar energy.

Sunbathing in the shade: Nude sunbathing in the shade provides you with light and air, but avoids sunburning yourself in the direct rays of the sun if you are just arriving at the beach, if your state of health requires some caution with overheating, or if you insist on continuing your sunbath right through the sundrenched hours of the day around noon.

The five-step method of safe sunning is another way you can control the effect of sunlight, especially if you are weakened from some illness or ailment and need to avoid, at least in the beginning, too much of the vigorous effect so easy to obtain from sun and sea:

1. Recline on an air mattress or chaise-lounge in the sun, but not in a draft.
2. Set up an umbrella to throw shade on your head only.
3. Cover up to your neck with a white, light-weight sheet. (White reflects much of the heat away from you.)
4. When you sweat, turn over on your stomach. Stay in that position until your back sweats.
5. Sprinkle yourself (or have someone rub you down) with tepid water, or, for refreshing more rapidly, use cool water.

Seven-day sun starter for safe tanning: A Swedish heliothera-puetist (specialist in using the sun as a means of treatment for certain ailments and disorders), Kristina R., used the following seven-day plan to safely reintroduce weakened, sun-starved convalescents to the summer sun:

Day 1: Five minutes of sun on the feet.

Day 2: Ten minutes of sun on the feet.
Five minutes on the lower legs.
(Expose feet and calves five minutes, then cover up the calves and give the feet an additional five minutes.)

Day 3: Fifteen minutes of sun on the feet.
Ten minutes on the calves.
Five minutes on the thighs.

Day 4: Twenty minutes of sun on the feet.
Fifteen minutes on the lower legs.
Ten minutes on the thighs.
Five minutes on the abdomen.

Day 5: Twenty-five minutes of sun on the feet.
Twenty minutes of sun on the lower legs.
Fifteen minutes of sun on the thighs.
Ten minutes of sun on the abdomen.
Five minutes of sun on the chest.

Day 6: Thirty minutes of sun on the feet.
Twenty-five minutes of sun on the lower legs.
Twenty minutes of sun on the thighs.
Fifteen minutes of sun on the abdomen.
Ten minutes of sun on the chest.
Five minutes of sun on the back.

By the end of the sixth day, you are receiving a total of thirty minutes of sun over the whole body. This was achieved by starting with five minutes on the back, then turning over on the back to expose the chest for ten minutes. Then you covered up the chest and gave the abdomen five minutes more (to make a total of fifteen minutes since it already has ten minutes). Then you covered up the abdomen and gave the thighs five minutes more (to make a total of twenty minutes since they already have fifteen minutes). Then you covered up the thighs and gave the lower legs five minutes (to make a total of twenty-five minutes since they already have twenty minutes). Then you covered up the lower legs, and gave the feet five minutes (to make a total of thirty minutes since they already have twenty-five minutes).

Day 7: Add fifteen minutes to the thirty-minute exposure to make a total of forty-five minutes of sun.

Add fifteen minutes more every day thereafter until you reach a total of three to six hours of sun daily, depending upon your condition, how hot the weather is, the time of day, and the season.

Kristina R. usually broke up the sunbath with a ten-minute rest in the shade between every hour of sun until tanning was well underway. This gave the patient's skin a chance to build up enough pigment (the tan) to protect itself from the sun's radiation.

ADVANTAGES OF SEASIDE VACATIONS AT MARINOTHERAPEUTIC SPAS AND RESORTS

Seaside spas along the North Sea and Baltic Sea coasts of Germany are part of a traditionally successful system of mineral, thermal and radioactive springs that contribute to excellent health care encompassing prevention, cure, convalescence and rehabilitation. The reputation of these spas and resorts — often well-equipped treatment centers staffed by specialists in the treatment of specific disorders — rests upon their effectiveness in not only providing unforgettable vacations, but also in dealing with chronic respiratory diseases, cardiovascular conditions, skin conditions, chronic disorders of the locomotor (movement, skeletal, muscular) system, female disorders, general debility, and children's medical problems. We just do not have the facilities like that here, so travel to them may be well worth the effort.

The addresses, kinds of seawater facilities in addition to the sea itself, and dates open are listed below for eighteen North Sea spas and ten Baltic Sea spas. These are followed by information on

Belgian, French, Spanish and Yugoslavian seaside health facilities. Health benefits from the Dead Sea are mentioned elsewhere in this book. With the reduced fares available today, a stay at one of these spas may really be more economical for you than you imagine. Although other countries also have highly effective spas and resorts for the successful treatment of many diseases and conditions, the western European ones are probably more accessible (in terms of money and distance) for most of us.

EIGHTEEN MARINOTHERAPEUTIC FACILITIES ON THE NORTH SEA

Address			Seawater pools (open all year unless otherwise noted)	
Zip	Place	Country	Outdoor	Indoor
2985	Baltrum	Germany	Yes	Yes
2972	Borkum	Germany	—	Yes
2242	Büsum	Germany	—	Yes
2190	Cuxhaven	Germany	Yes (April to October)	Yes
2192	Helgoland	Germany	Yes	—
2983	Juist	Germany	—	Yes
2941	Langeoog	Germany	—	Yes
2279	Norddorf auf Amrum	Germany	Yes	Yes
2982	Norderney	Germany	Yes	Yes
2252	St. Peter-Ording	Germany	—	Yes
2941	Spiekeroog	Germany	—	—
2946	Wangerooge	Germany	Yes (May to September)	Yes
2283	Wennigstedt auf Sylt	Germany	—	—
2280	Westerland auf Sylt	Germany	—	(closed Nov. 15 to Dec. 15)
2940	Wilhelmshaven	Germany	—	—
2278	Wittdün auf Amrum	Germany	Yes	Yes
2270	Wyk auf Föhr	Germany	—	Yes
2271	Utersum auf Föhr	Germany	—	—

TEN MARINOTHERAPEUTIC SPAS AND RESORTS
ON THE BALTIC SEA

Address			Seawater pools (open all year unless otherwise noted)	
Zip	Place	Country	Outdoor	Indoor
2448	Burg auf Fehmarn	Germany	—	Yes
2435	Dahme	Germany	Yes (April to September)	—
2330	Eckernförde	Germany	—	Yes, plus whirlpool
2392	Glücksburg	Germany	—	Yes, plus whirlpool
2433	Gromitz	Germany	Yes	Yes, plus surf bath
2409	Haffkrug-Scharbeutz	Germany	—	Yes, plus surf bath
2436	Kellenhusen	Germany	—	—
2304	Laboe	Germany	—	Yes
2408	Timmendorfer Strand/Niendorf	Germany	Yes	Yes
2400	Travemünde	Germany	Yes	Yes

A THERMAL INSTITUTE ON THE BELGIAN COAST

Ostend offers hot (95°F) seawater pools, mud baths, mineral and seawater baths, underwater massage, and therapy with other means (aerosols, shortwaves, ultrasound light, infrared light, galvanic-faradaic current), plus all the amenities of a beach holiday spot. Address: Official Tourist Information Bureau, Wapenplein, 8400 Ostend, Belgium.

FIFTEEN THALASSOTHERAPEUTIC FACILITIES
ON THE ATLANTIC OCEAN
AND THE MEDITERRANEAN SEA

Thalassotherapy involves the use of warmed seawater baths (some even with seaweeds in the water), gargles, sprays, jets and douches, sunshine, seacoast climate, physiotherapy and massages with seawater.

Seawater treatment, according to the spokesman for all of France's thalassotherapeutic centers:

1. Stimulates the body's defenses
2. Tones up the circulation
3. Facilitates elimination of the body's toxic wastes
4. Orchestrates proper cooperation among the body's hormones

The French resorts in the list which follows use thalassotherapy to successfully relieve sufferers of the following conditions: Chronic rheumatism or arthrosis with its painful swelling, contractions, loss of muscular flexibility, and stiffness which can afflict joints and their surrounding tissues. Other conditions treated are cellulitis, gout, dry dermatitis, poor venous circulation in the legs, painful symptoms of displaced vertebrae and slipped discs, paralysis, Parkinson's disease, bone/joint degeneration in the elderly (who are not otherwise in too fragile a state for hot seawater bathing), and painfully difficult breathing caused by the stiff joints connecting the breastbone with the ribs. Also, thalassotherapy is used for recuperation from accidents and surgery, as well as from overwrought conditions caused by overexertion and the stress of urban life. Persons, however, who have infectious diseases, especially pulmonary tuberculosis, certain kinds of heart and kidney insufficiency, oozing dermatitis or various mental disorders, are usually not advised to take this kind of treatment.

The French thalassotherapeutic centers listed below are located in the *stimulating climate near the English Channel:*

*   Thermes Marins, Rue Edmond-Blanc, 14800 Deauville (Calvados).
*   Cure Marine Siouville, Rue Marcel Grillard, 50340 Siouville-Hague (Manche).
*   Institut de Thalassothérapie de la Côte d'Opale, Front de Mer, 62520 Le Touquet (Pas-de-Calais).
*   Cures Marines de Trouville, Promenade des Planches, 14360 Trouville (Calvados).

The centers listed below are located in the *mildly bracing climate of Brittany:*

*   Centre de Cure Marine de la Baie de Treboul-Douarnenez, B.P. 4, 29100 Douarnenez (Finistère).

- Institut de Thalassothérapie de Quiberon, B.P. 41, Quiberon (Morbihan).
- Centre de Thalassothérapie-Rheumatologie Rock-Roum, B.P. 28, 29211 Roscoff (Finistère).
- Centre de Thalassothérapie-Readaptation Fonctionelle Ker Lena, 29211 Roscoff (Finistère).
- Thermes Marins, 100 Bd Hébert, B.P. 32, 35401 Saint-Malo Parame (Ille-et-Vilaine).

Centers in a more *southerly, "sedative" climate* are:

- Institut de Thalassothérapie Neptune, B.P. 1, 17740 Sainte-Marie-de-Re, Ile de Ré (Charente-Maritime).
- Institut de Thalassothérapie d'Oleron, Plage de Gatseau, 17370 Saint-Trojan-les-Bains, Ile d'Oléron (Charente-Maritime).

Centers in an *even more "sedative" climate* are:

- Bellamar, Port Canto, 06400 Cannes (Alpes-Maritimes).
- Thermes Marins, Avenue Wilson, 13600 La Ciotat (Bouches-du-Rhône).
- Institut de Thalassothérapie de Porticcio, 20000 Porticcio (Corsica).
- Institut Marin La Calanco, B.P. 162, 83700 Saint-Raphael (Var).

TWO SPANISH THALASSOTHERAPEUTIC AND HELIOTHERAPEUTIC CENTERS

Thalassotherapy (use of seawater and seacoast climate) and *heliotherapy* (use of the curative powers of the sun) are the specialties at the *Centro Helioterápico Canario* — sun-warmed sand baths sprinkled with fresh seawater, and hot seawater showers. The sand contains magnetite (an iron oxide that can be magnetized, and then called lodestone) and ferrotitanic constituents, that is, iron and titanium. Conditions successfully treated here include joint diseases, rheumatism, joint conditions following injuries or surgery, general detoxification of the body, and obesity. Full address: Centro Helioterápico Canario, Maspalmas Costa Canaria, Edificio Cantabria, Paso de Chil, 282, Las Palmas de Gran Canario, Spain.

Another center — *Centro de Termalismo y Recuperación Funcional* — features jet showers, seaweed and marine mud baths, sun and air bathing, sand baths, and massage with seawater. Conditions successfully treated here include rheumatic conditions, neurologic disorders, obesity, and the ravages of aging. Rehabilitation and recuperation, such as following injuries, are important activities here. Full address: Centro de Termalismo y Recuperación Funcional, Benicasim (Castellón de la Plana), Spain.

RADIOACTIVE SEA MUD AND SALT WATER
ON THE ADRIATIC SEA

The Yugoslavian seacoast resort of Igalo offers sea mud that is organic, mineral and slightly radioactive. Conditions successfully treated here include rheumatological, neurological, psychosomatic, heart-lung, vascular, bone and joint, and female disorders. Full address: Zavod za fizikalnu medicinu i rehabilitaci ju Miloševic, 81347 Igalo, Yugoslavia.

13

How to Enjoy the Benefits
of Seawater
and Other Curative Baths at Home

"Water is miraculous," Dr. Ilya, the hydrotherapeutic director of the seaside resort, said as he clamped his big hand down on my shoulder. "Include *all* water cures in your sea book. Freshwater, seawater, mineral spring water, thermal springs, it's all connected." So, to bridge over from the water in the sea to the water in your bathtub at home, here are several ways to mix up a seawater-like bath at home.

HOW TO COLLECT AND CONDITION
NATURAL SEAWATER

If you have any doubt as to how clean your coastal water may be, here are a few ways that an experienced aquarist, Dr. A., clears up the coastal water he collects and takes home for his marine aquarium, which is populated with quite delicate little animals that could not survive the slightest change in water quality:

1. Stores a tubful of the seawater in total darkness for at least two weeks. During this time the plankton or microscopic larval creatures die and sink to the bottom; and after a temporary increase in bacteria, about three to ten days, the water becomes clear and is free of living organisms (whose residue stays behind as a brown sediment on the bottom when you carefully pour off or dip out the clear water above).

2. Heats the seawater to at least 140° F, then lets it stand for two days until the residue of any microscopic organisms in it settles out on the bottom. Dr. A. heats his water in glass or inert plastic containers because his delicate fish cannot tolerate the water if he heats it in metal containers. However, the metal of ordinary kitchen pots should not hurt human beings who bathe in water that was boiled in them.

HOW TO USE MARINE SALT
FOR BATHS

For bathing in "semi-natural" seawater at home, dried natural marine salt, or sea salt, has been used in quantities as low as half a pound of salt to one bathtub of tapwater, and as much as two or even four pounds of salt for each tubful of water. Some people have even used stronger solutions of natural marine salt for bathing their hands, feet or on compresses over painful joints, but only after checking first with their physicians.

BATH ADDITIVES TO MAKE
SYNTHETIC SEAWATER AT HOME

The experience of aquarium curators and countless amateur aquarists and marine biologists has been that once seawater is dehydrated, it may be reconstituted by adding water...but it never again supports all of the marine life it once did before being processed. For the purposes of simulating seawater in a bathtub, however, so-called synthetic seasalts may serve well enough.

Several of these synthetic mixes have proven useful in providing artificial seawater for raising marine creatures under laboratory or aquarium conditions. One, for example, contains twenty-three elements and inorganic substances: chlorine, sodium, sulfate, magnesium, potassium, calcium, bicarbonate, boron, bromine, strontium, phosphate, manganese, molybdenum, sulfur, lithium, rubidium, iodine, aluminum, zinc, vanadium, cobalt, iron and copper. Synthetic seawater or marine salts are sold in aquarium supply houses and pet shops.

Commercially available artificial kidney fluid, too, may have some use as a seawater substitute. This fluid, or dialysate, is pumped through the kidney machine used to "wash the blood" of people with non-functioning or only poorly functioning kidneys, or without any kidneys at all. These dialysate mixes contain vital minerals which, when added to fresh water, make up a seawater-like bath which simulates the mineral content of the blood. (Remember that our blood and the seas have a common ancestry!) A typical dialysate or artificial kidney fluid may contain sodium, chloride, calcium, magnesium, acetate, and potassium. (For a seawater bath, we would not be interested in the dialysate mixes that also contain glucose, since seawater does not contain it.) Dialysate mixes are available from Travenol, Cobe, Mallinckrodt, Renal Systems, Extracorporeal, and other firms.

Simulated seawater may be used in place of freshwater from the tap for many of the kinds of baths and soaks described below.

THE ADVANTAGE OF HOT AND COLD BATHS

A spa physician, Dr. von G., enumerated the following four benefits of warm baths:

1. Increases peristalsis (the rhythmic surging which propels food along the gastrointestinal tract).
2. Increases secretion of gastric and digestive juices.
3. Reduces pain.
4. Increases permeability of the skin to allow passage of ions (electrically charged particles) liberated by substances dissolved in the bath water.

Dr. von G.'s experience with using baths for treating his patients, and knowledge gained from physiological experiments showed that:

1. Blood pressure drops in warm baths, but rises in either very hot or very cold baths.
2. Overly hot baths increase the activity of the heart, but can lead, although rarely, in certain circumstances, to circulatory collapse even in apparently healthy bathers.

3. Partial baths are safer than full ones for persons with serious circulatory conditions because the heat or cold is applied to only *part* of the body, thus providing a milder effect that does not jolt the system.

4. Cold baths lead to over-acidity of the blood in some diabetic patients, and would therefore be unfavorable for such persons.

WHY JAPANESE WOMEN HAVE LESS BREAST CANCER

The extremely low amount of breast cancer in Japanese women, according to a physician who has studied the problem, may be due to the long, hot baths (around 120° F or higher) they take, and not necessarily or completely to their lack of many of the processed foods, meats and fats on which we gorge ourselves in our western diet. The body's immunity mechanisms, it was thought, may be stimulated by these very hot baths in which Japanese women relax along with their families, all submerged up to their necks.

Caution: As mentioned elsewhere in this book, very hot (or very cold) baths are not good for everyone. Very hot baths are not good for persons not used to them, or persons with heart or certain other conditions.

HOW WET GRASS INCREASES TONE AND VITALITY

Beginning at the grass-roots level, one can run barefoot through grass moist with early morning dew, or stroll barefoot over pebbles in a babbling brook, or sit on the bank of a river or a boat landing and dangle both feet in the water. This barefoot treatment not only tones you up in general, but relaxes your tense, nervous body, and then revitalizes it. Everything benefits from such a grass-roots approach, including the digestion and one's whole mental outlook. Father Sebastian Kneipp, a German priest and widely recognized "water doctor" of the nineteenth century, had his patients traipsing like this through early morning dew and splashing about like children in pools and streams.

HOW TO BATHE TO INCREASE TONE, RESISTANCE TO DISEASE, KIDNEY FUNCTION, AND TO FIGHT OBESITY, INSOMNIA, COLDS, RHEUMATISM, LUMBAGO, CRAMPS, STONES AND HEMORRHOIDAL PAIN

A full bath or shower builds good body tone and resistance to minor indispositions (colds, infections, fatigue). The stimulation of the skin caused by washing and the temperature of the water goes deeper than just the skin; it also affects the excretory function of the kidneys (that is how salt gets into our sweat) and the respiratory function of the lungs (because we breathe through the pores of our skin).

Obese persons or those with high fever may benefit from cold baths (lasting only a few seconds!), but this shock is not for persons with kidney or heart conditions, or for those in a weakened state. Warm baths (thirty seconds) combat insomnia. Hot baths (fifteen minutes), although not suitable for persons with heart conditions, are good for countering a beginning cold, rheumatism, lumbago, cramps, colic from stones, or hemorrhoidal pain. A cold splash or shower *after* a hot or warm bath is rather pleasant and does not shock most people. In fact, it closes the pores of the skin and protects against chilling when leaving the bath. Scandinavians who run out of a *sauna* (a dry, hot-air bath made by dashing water over hot rocks, usually in a specially built cabin) and then take a cold dip or roll in the snow do not usually shiver — if they come right inside the house and dress warmly. A warm drink helps. So does climbing right into a bed, and covering up with a blanket or feather quilt.

HOW TO IMPROVE CIRCULATION FOR BEDRIDDEN PERSONS

A partial bath, or bed-bath, and mild rubbing with a washcloth not only cleanses persons confined to bed but, more importantly, promotes good blood circulation and refreshes the patient physically and mentally. This rubbing and washing also helps prevent the bedsores caused by constant pressure on the skin of persons confined to a bed or a wheelchair.

Wash one arm vigorously, dry it by rubbing briskly, and then cover it with a sheet or blanket to prevent chilling. Then move on to the other arm, and so on until the whole body has been washed, dried, and covered piece by piece.

HOW TO APPLY THERMAL PACKS
FOR RELIEVING PAIN, CHEST INFECTIONS,
PHLEBITIS, GASTROINTESTINAL AND HEART
CONDITIONS, INSOMNIA, HEADACHE
AND HIGH BLOOD PRESSURE

For laryngitis, pharyngitis and other painfully inflamed throat conditions, soak a linen cloth in cold water, wring it out, fold it into a larger dry, woolen cloth so that none of the wrung-out linen is opened to the air, and wrap this cool, linen and wool pack around the neck. Some alleviation will occur before the pack warms up and dries out in about an hour or so; then, soak the linen again and re-apply, if necessary. If the body heat does not warm up the pack enough, a hot-water bottle should be laid on the pack. It is this cool-warm action that is beneficial. The cool linen at first causes the blood vessels to contract, but they begin to dilate as the wool warms up; this not only relieves pain but actually affects circulation and helps the body to overcome infection.

Bronchitis, pneumonia and dry pleurisy are helped by chest wrappings prepared like the throat wrappings described above.

Phlebitis and even insomnia and headache can be helped by wrapping the calves of the legs.

A large wrapping on the abdomen may afford relief in gastro-intestinal and heart conditions, high blood pressure and insomnia.

HOW TO PROMOTE HEALING
AND LESSEN PAIN WITH COMPRESSES

The application of hot compresses helps promote healing and also alleviates pain caused by gallstones, kidney stones, abdominal (especially menstrual) cramps, arthritis, rheumatism, gout, furuncles, bronchitis and other chest infections.

Prepare hot compresses by soaking a linen cloth in hot water, and wringing it out before applying it to the skin. It is not always a good idea to use gloves or tongs for protecting your hands when wringing out the hot water, because the cloth might be too hot for the skin and you will not be able to feel that heat if you protect your hands. After you have placed the compress, cover it with a second, woolen cloth and leave it on for about thirty to sixty minutes. Re-

fresh the skin by sponging or wiping it with cool water before applying another hot compress.

The application of cold compresses may alleviate pain when
hot compresses do not help. The pain of burns, in particular, is
relieved by plunging the burned part, if possible, into iced water;
otherwise, iced-water compresses are quite effective.

HOW TO WASH EYES TO RELIEVE INFLAMMATION

Conjunctivitis or eye inflammation is relieved by ducking the
face in a basin of clean, cool water and winking the eyes several
times under water, coming up for air, and then repeating the winking once again under water.

HOW TO SPRAY WATER TO RELIEVE HEADACHE, INSOMNIA AND RHEUMATISM

A steady stream of cold water sprayed from the feet up to the
calves, continued on up to the knees, and then up to the hips and
down again, relieves headache (like the cool leg wrapping described
above). Greater stimulatory effect may be had by continuing the
stream of water up the back, but this is too invigorating for weakened
or elderly people, or for those with heart conditions. For these persons, direct the water in a milder way — up and down the arms
(thirty seconds) — to help them overcome insomnia, or to relieve
rheumatic pain in the arms or shoulders. The colder the water, the
more rapidly a sensation of warmth follows.

HOW TO BATHE TO RELIEVE HEMORRHOIDS, REGULATE MENSTRUATION, AND ALLEVIATE THE PAIN OF STONES

Sitz bath: Fill a bathtub with enough water to reach just below
your belly button. Now you have a *sitz* bath just deep enough to sit
in. (*Sitz* is German for sit or sitting.) A hot *sitz* bath soothes hemorrhoidal and other pains; a cold one helps stimulate normal function
in the lower abdomen, including regulation of menstrual irregular-
ities; a hot one (for five minutes) followed by a cold one (for ten
seconds) may alleviate the pain of stones.

Bidet douche: The bidet (often found as a porcelain bathroom
fixture in Europe and Latin America, in South Florida houses built
by Cuban contractors, and elsewhere) is a jet-spray douche over

which one sits, like on a toilet bowl. It provides a fine means of reducing pain in swollen hemorrhoid tissues, and can be used as an alternative to sitting in a hot *sitz* bath for relieving painful hemorrhoids. When using the jet-spray, start with a fine, warm spray; then gradually increase the temperature and pressure until a comfortable spray is obtained which relieves the aching hemorrhoids.

HOW TO BATHE FOR HEAD-TO-TOE RELIEF

Dangle your feet and lower legs in cold water for one to two minutes to relieve excess foot sweating, pain from varicose veins, and foot pains, especially those caused by flat feet.

Dangle your feet and legs in hot water for ten to twenty minutes to alleviate eye, ear, and nasal conditions, bronchitis, migraine headache and asthmatic attacks.

HOW TO NORMALIZE IRREGULAR HEART ACTION

A hotel physician, Dr. L., did not care to use any more medication on himself (or anyone else, for that matter) than absolutely necessary. He normalized his own irregular heart beat, due to nervousness, by placing on his chest, just over his heart, a square of linen cloth soaked in cold (40° F) water. Over that he laid a rubberized ice bag filled with cold water, holding it all in place with a strip of flannel tied around his chest. Dr. L. claimed that this helped (even when digitalis did not) some of his weakened patients who had overly rapid heart action. He said he also used it successfully to protect the heart of patients with typhoid fever.

HOW HOT WATER SOOTHES AN IRRITATED STOMACH

Dr. Ilya soothed yet stimulated his irritable, nervous and sometimes inflamed stomach by drinking two to three glasses of hot water — hot enough to drink by only sipping — from thirty to sixty minutes before a meal.

HOW TO EASE LUMBAGO AND SCIATIC PAINS

A Danish masseuse, Erna L., relieved the lumbago and sciatic pains of many of her older clients by applying hot compresses in the following way:

1. Rub Vaseline or any other petrolatum jelly on the affected part.
2. Soak and then wring out two strips of flannel in boiling water and apply. If it is too hot, gradually build up to it by first applying a very warm compress, then a hotter one, and so on until you get the hottest one that can be tolerated without actually burning the skin.
3. Lay a blanket over the flannel to keep the heat in.
4. Soak the flannel again and reapply about every fifteen minutes until sweating breaks out. Then give the skin time to recuperate awhile before starting with new applications.
5. When the pain subsides, uncover the affected part, rub it dry quickly, or else massage it with lukewarm water (75° F).

HERBAL BATH ADDITIVES
FOR ADDED CURATIVE AND PREVENTIVE EFFECTS

In addition to the aforementioned variety in water temperature, parts of the body bathed, and utilization of alternating hot and cold water, one can also add supplements to a bath or to compresses. A hot, soapy bath, for example, has been given to persons with measles or scarlet fever for stimulating skin and for drawing disease-causing substances outward. Herbal supplements in the bath provide active ingredients that actually enter the body through the skin, just as the minerals in seawater penetrate the skin to exert some of their solutory effect when we wade along in the surf. The home bather can turn common plants into alleviating, beautifying and nutritive baths. For example, clover in the bath beautifies the skin and alleviates itching. Willow bark contains an aspirin-like substance that helps relieve the pain of rheumatism, the discomfort of eczema, festering ulcers, and flaking skin. Because of the importance attached to such herbal baths, especially abroad, by physicians and experienced people who know how to care for themselves, here is an example of an already prepared herbal bath. *Bath for promoting circulation and alleviating varicosed veins* either in the legs or in the rectum (hemorrhoids, too, are varicosed veins) contains chamomile, oak, yarrow, horse chestnut, fir, wheat germ, soya, yeast and chlorophyll. This bath is taken every two or three days for fifteen to twenty minutes at a little less than body temperature, that is, about 86° F instead of at 98 or 99° F. If veins are acutely inflamed or there are varicose ulcers, then your physician should approve your taking this bath. Likewise, if you suffer from a disease that makes you feverish, have tuberculosis, have serious cardiovascular problems, or have high blood pressure, then your physician should approve your taking any of the above baths before you take them, according to the firm that packages these plant baths (Dr. Otto Greither, 8206 Bruckmühl/ Oberbayern, Germany).

If you prefer to prepare baths from raw plant materials you collect yourself, or which you can purchase at shops that stock health products, the following sections will guide you.

Prepare a full bath for an adult, as a general rule, by adding half to a full pound of a plant supplement (such as the ones recommended following this section) to the water. For children, persons with a delicate constitution, and persons in a weakened condition use less plant material. Part of the secret in helping living organisms — whether people, dogs, or food-crop plants — to overcome disease, or in helping them to be strong, healthy, and resistant to disease, is to *build* and *develop,* rather than giving a shock-dose of a powerful drug and expecting an instant miracle of recuperation. Strong medicine does not always cure more quickly, and it may even harm a person already weakened by illness or who has a delicate constitution. Strong medicine, such as big doses of a plant in a bath or overly strenuous steam baths, are for strong people — not delicate ones. "Delicate," however, does not necessarily mean puny, skinny, or small. Some small, apparently puny people may be quite resistant and tough constitutionally. A large football star may crumble under an illness that hardly fazes a seemingly unfit, scrawny little fellow. (Fitness means the ability to adjust to environmental changes so as to survive...rolling with the punches or bending like the palm tree in a hurricane when stronger hardwood trees are uprooted and snapped in two.) The one-half to one pound of plant material per full bath recommended above, then, is for the average adult in fairly good general health (except, of course, for the ailment being treated). Some of the following baths, however, use greater or lesser amounts, as indicated where applicable.

Many of these plant materials may be purchased at health food stores, grocery stores, spice shops or some pharmacies. Refer to Chapter 14 for specific instructions on how to handle plant materials and how to make the teas, infusions and decoctions that go into the baths described below.

1. *Balsam poplar tree or tacamahac* — A warm footbath made from bark decoction helps overcome malodorous foot sweat.

2. *Barley* — A warm bath containing a barley decoction reduces fever and alleviates skin conditions. Applications of wrappings or compresses soaked in barley water may be used instead of the full bath.

Hot barley soup is perhaps much better known than the cool, milky white barley-water drink served over the counter in Central American bars. Barley is a nourishing food that quenches thirst, provides vitamins (A,B,D and E), increases blood pressure to a healthy level and soothes skin conditions. Several drinks of barley water loosen phlegm in the moist, congestive condition associated with colds. Frequent, refreshing drinks of it relieve chronic diarrhea, stones, liver and spleen conditions and anemia. For gout and neurasthenia, an inside-outside course of barley may help: drink barley water mixed with malt (malt is germinated barley) and apply packs of warm barley water to the painful spots.

3. *Birch tree* — A warm footbath from bark relieves foot sweat and various skin conditions. Shampoos of tea from leaves, bark, buds or sap have helped to clear up various hair and scalp conditions.

4. *Bran* — A warm bath from a bran decoction alleviates rheumatism, gout, and some skin irritations.

5. *Calamus or sweet flag* — A warm bath containing a decoction made from half a gram to two grams of powdered root has helped strengthen sickly children. Collect the root in the fall or spring, and dry gently in an oven or warm, dry place.

Fir trees in general — A warm footbath containing a decoction of needles, bark and fruit invigorates the whole body and relieves tired feet; frequent, warm baths containing a three-hour decoction of fir buds invigorate elderly and weakened bathers. Different kinds of pines, spruces, firs and larches are often used interchangeably for obtaining the benefits described below.

6. *Silver fir* — A warm bath containing a one-hour decoction of fir needles has helped to strengthen lungs and impart a feeling of well-being.

7. *Spruce fir* — A warm bath containing a two-hour decoction

of four pounds of twigs (strain out the twigs) has alleviated chest ailments and difficult breathing, as well as skin infections, rheumatism and gout.

8. *Larch* — A warm bath containing a decoction of fresh twigs has alleviated skin ulcers, abscesses and boils.

9. *Hemp* — A warm eyewash made from a decoction of hemp foliage has reportedly helped clear up corneal flecks and cloudiness, as well as reduce scintillations (seeing flashes or sparks).

10. *Honeysuckle* — A warm eyewash made from an infusion of honeysuckle flowers has soothed inflamed, tired eyes.

11. *Horse chestnut* — A warm decoction of horse chestnut bark used as a wet compress has helped soothe gangrenous wounds.

12. *Horsetail grass* — A warm *sitz* bath containing a decoction of horsetail grass has helped relieve kidney and bladder ailments, and has eased urination when it was difficult; it has also reportedly been used in a footbath to alleviate foot ulcers and osteitis (bone inflammation).

13. *Juniper* — Warm baths containing a four-hour decoction of juniper twigs and stinging nettle leaves alleviate gout, rheumatism and sciatic pains.

14. *Lignum vitae* — Massage a hot bark decoction into the site affected by rheumatism to relieve pain.

15. *Mullein* — Warm baths or soaks containing mullein leaf tea have been used to control fevers, reduce the pain of sprains, relieve sore feet and rheumatic pains in the legs, and alleviate hemorrhoidal pain. Dried mullein leaves wrapped in corn husks, by the way, have been smoked to relieve asthma.

16. *Oats* — Warm baths containing a decoction of one quart of oats in two quarts of water (boiled down until only one quart of water is left) have been used for rheumatism, diabetes, and children with intestinal problems (especially intestinal flu).

17. *Oat straw* — A warm bath containing a decoction of oat straw has been used to alleviate the discomfort of urinary tract conditions (stones, etc.), gout, rheumatism, sweating feet, and eczema; hot compresses soaked in oat straw have been used for the relief of lower abdominal cramps.

18. *Oak* — A warm bath containing a decoction of oak bark has helped clear up eczema; a hot footbath containing a decoction of oak fruit plus bark invigorates tired, aching feet.

19. *Peppermint* — A warm bath containing peppermint leaf

tea refreshes and stimulates the whole body; peppermint, thyme and rosemary in a warm bath strengthens the body and relieves physical and mental exhaustion.

20.   *Spanish or Florida moss* — A hot bath containing a decoction of Spanish moss has helped relieve the discomfort of rheumatism and hemorrhoids.

21.   *Thyme* — A warm bath containing thyme tea acts antiseptically, stimulates body functions, and helps heal bruises, sprains and swollen injuries.

22.   *Walnut* — A warm bath containing a decoction of walnut tree bark and fruit relieves tired, aching feet; a leaf decoction helps heal stubborn wounds and bone infections.

23.   *Willow* — A warm bath of bark decoction has been used for eczema and festering ulcers; flaking skin has reportedly been helped by wet compresses of bark decoction.

24.   *Wonderberry or chinaberry* — A warm bath containing leaf or fruit infusion, or trunk or root decoction, has been used to relieve eczema and other skin conditions. (Half a bushel of wonderberry fruit mashed in fifteen gallons of water, by the way, protects garden plants from black grubs and cutworms!)

14

Preparation of Teas, Infusions and Decoctions for Healing Baths

Many of the curative and preventive baths described in the foregoing chapter were made with teas or infusions and decoctions from vegetables, spices and condiments, fruits, trees and various other plant matter. In many cases, then, the first step in making a bath additive is to make a tea, or decoction, which is then poured into the bathtub of water. People also drink teas and decoctions or soak compresses with them for use as wound dressings. Keep in mind, however, that some "teas" should *not* be drunk, but used only externally for compresses or in baths.

WHEN TO COLLECT CURATIVE PLANTS

The Medieval plant collectors who were advised to "take by the light of the full moon but before the first dew, the underground part of a full-grown..." were usually not being mystified with meaningless hokus-pokus, for there are indeed good and bad times for collecting medicinal plants. Time of collection can influence a plant's usefulness or its poisonousness. The normally very sweet-tasting persimmon is an example of seasonal change in plant contents: bite into an unripe persimmon and feel your lips pucker up from the astringent effect of the unripe fruit!

The time of collection varies according to the part of the plant being taken. Roots are best gathered in the spring before the plant's vegetative processes begin and the sap rises, or just after these processes end in the autumn after the leaves are dry. Leaves should be taken when the flowers are developing, before the fruit and seeds mature. Flowers are best plucked before or just at pollination time. Fruits should be full-grown but not quite ripe. Seeds should be gathered when they are fully mature.

HOW TO PRESERVE
THE CURATIVE INGREDIENTS OF PLANTS

Bark: After cleaning off and discarding the outer portion of bark, cut up the remainder into chunks and store in a dry place.

Roots: Dry in an oven after slicing so that the heat can penetrate well.

Seeds: Dry on screens to allow a free current of air to pass up between the seeds.

Berries and fruits: Spread or hang berries and fruits in a cool, dry place. Pulpy fruit, however, should be gently heated in an oven.

Leaves: Dry leaves rapidly by hanging or spreading them so that a current of air passes through them.

Flowers: Dry in a darkened room.

Store dried materials in wooden boxes or other closed containers that protect them against insects, moisture and light.

HOW TO PREPARE
FRESH JUICE TO USE IN TEAS AND BATHS

Pack finely diced fresh plant parts into the middle part of a fine-mesh silk or nylon stocking, then wring both ends simultaneously to extraot the juice.

HOW TO MAKE TEAS, INFUSIONS
AND DECOCTIONS AS BATH ADDITIVES

Teas and infusions are made by steeping. Decoctions are made by heating more vigorously (that is, by thorough boiling) to extract more ingredients from tougher, harder plant parts.

Use glass or earthenware vessels for heating to avoid any reaction of plant substances with the metal of common kitchen utensils.

Steep soft parts (flowers, leaves, petals) by dousing them with boiling water, but do not boil the parts directly, for ten to fifteen minutes in a cup topped with a saucer or other device to keep the heat and volatile oils from escaping.

Boil hard parts (roots, inner and outer barks, twigs, stalks, seeds) about ten minutes in ten times the amount of water that it takes to just cover them.

If the substance is dry, it may be necessary to beat or bruise several ounces of it before boiling to extract the active ingredients. If the substance is fresh, slice it so that the maximum surface area is exposed to the boiling water. A reserve of materials may be kept by pounding and crushing thoroughly dried parts and storing the powder obtained in amber bottles until needed.

Not all plant substances can be successfully boiled; the active ingredient may be volatile at boiling heat and pass off as vapor, or it may be changed to an undesirable product.

Prepare only the amount of liquid needed for immediate use, and do not keep teas, infusions or decoctions more than a day or so; unfavorable chemical changes may occur that make the liquid unfit for use.

Store only dried parts of the plants or powders which you have prepared. Otherwise, mold and bacteria may gain a foothold and ruin the material, or undesirable chemical changes may occur just as in the liquid.

How to ferment tea: Fermentation changes green tea to black tea (that is, the usual Chinese, Indian, Ceylonese and Japanese kinds of tea), thereby changing the color of the leaves, activating certain substances, and imparting a characteristic aroma. Fermentation also contributes to odixation of some of the tannin in the leaves, thus making the tea milder and less astringent.

Let the leaves (of whatever plant you are making into tea) wilt a day or so — perhaps about forty hours — then roll and keep them under a moist linen cloth for another day or so to ferment. Then dry them quickly to prevent any microorganisms from gaining a foothold, and either ruining the flavor or building up substances that make the tea unfit or unsafe to drink.

WHY YOU SHOULD NOT MISTRUST
ALL REMEDIES THAT SEEM TO CURE TOO MUCH

Some remedies work for some people some of the time. Other remedies always work for some people. And still other remedies always work for everyone. Can we believe in a particular herbal bath or other remedy that is reported to relieve several, apparently different ailments? Yes, it may indeed do just that. Many connections — some as yet still poorly understood or even totally unsuspected — exist between seemingly unrelated parts and functions of our body. Who has not seen cold, wet feet lead to a terrible head cold? Or a toothache turn into a backache? The Oriental art of acupuncture has clearly shown us that a needle prick, or perhaps mere pressure by a finger, at one spot on the body leads to sometimes spectacular effects at other spots. So, you certainly can believe that dangling your feet and legs in hot water can relieve a headache as well as bronchitis and asthma, too. And that horsetail grass in your bath can alleviate urinary tract conditions as well as clear up foot ulcers. And that the earth's waters, especially the seas, provide the health and relief outlined in this book.

15

Far Eastern Sea Products
Available in the U.S.A.

The Far Eastern marine products distributed for many manufacturers by *Japan Food Corporation* (P.O. Box 6096; Long Island City, New York 11106) include the following canned items:

- Boiled abalone.
- Cut-up abalone tidbits.
- "Red clams" or arkshells.
- Skewered arkshells.
- "Short-necked clams" or carpet shells.
- Boiled baby clams.
- Smoked baby clams.
- Cuttlefish.
- Squid.
- Boiled eel.
- Broiled eel.
- Boiled eel heads.
- *Nerisei-hin* — a general term for kneaded fish products, including the following:
  - *Chikuwa* — popsicle-like cylinder of scorched, kneaded, jellied fish around a stick.

- *Kamaboko* — jellified fish meat loaf prepared by heating kneaded fish meat plus salt, sugar, *mirin* (sweet fermented brew from rice), and several other ingredients.
- *Satsuma age* — fried kamaboko, or *goboiri tempura* is made with burdock. (Burdock, by the way, has been used in the form of a tea, made from five grams of the root, for clearing up eruptions, festered wounds, abscesses, boils, gout, rheumatism, mange or scurf, blisters in the mouth or on the lips; the tea was applied directly on the skin or else drunk. Oil expressed from the burdock root has also been rubbed into the scalp to counter loss of hair.)

- Mackerel in tomato sauce.
- Mackerel in vegetable oil.
- Mackerel in its natural oil.
- Mackerel with bean paste.
- Mackerel boiled in water.
- Octopus.
- Boiled oysters.
- Smoked oysters.
- Sardines (pilchard or Pacific sardines).
- Saury in water.
- Saury *kabayaki* — translated by the distributor as baked saury; *kabayaki* style, however, can also mean, especially for eels, splitting, steaming, then broiling with repeated dunking into *tare* (soy sauce, sugar, mirin, and various other ingredients).
- Shark-fin soup.
- Skewered Korean top shells.
- Crabmeat.
- Bite-size tuna hors d'oeuvres (three kinds: to go with beer, to go with sake rice wine, or to go with hard liquor).
- *Kombu* (also spelled *konbu*) — *Laminaria* and other species of brown seaweed or tangle.

The Japan Food Corporation also distributes dry sea products, which include:

- Smoked cuttlefish.
- *Surume* — cuttlefish or squid, cleaned of entrails and eyes, split and dried.
- Shrimp.

- Sea cucumber — a cucumber-like bottom-dwelling animal which ejects its insides when disturbed...and then regenerates another set of insides! The raw entrails of some sea cucumbers are eaten as delicacies. Also called *trepang* (when dried), *bêche de mer* and sea slug.
- Sardines *sakuraboshi* style — split, soaked in soy sauce, sugar and *mirin* — or else in salt, sugar, millet jelly and agar — then dried.
- Whole sardines.
- Bonito (that is, oceanic or stripe-bellied bonito) or skipjack flakes. (The viscera of skipjack, by the way, are used to produce insulin industrially. Skipjack liver oil is particularly rich in vitamin D.)
- Bonito (with the same synonyms as above) powder for soup stock.
- Saury *hamayabi* style — skewered, toasted and dried.
- Saury *mirinboshi* style — similar to *sakuraboshi* style, described for the dried sardine *sakuraboshi* above.
- Japanese tuna sticks or *katsuobushi* condiment or soup stock — long dried sticks of boned, boiled, smouldered, dried and shaped Japanese tuna (or skipjack) meat, enzymatically defatted by the use of molds.
- Shredded, boned cod.
- Smoked cod fillets.
- Baked cod.
- Hard-smoked cod.
- Smoked octopus.
- Herring with *mirin* sauce (see description of *mirin* above).
- Smoked chum salmon.
- Cuttlefish strips.

Frozen sea products, too, are distributed by Japan Food Corporation:

- *Kamaboko* — jellied fish as described above, under canned products.
- *Chikuwa* — popsickle-like jellied fish as described above.
- Tempura — fried *kamaboko*.
- Shrimp.
- Abalone.
- "Red clams" or arkshells.
- Conger eel.

- Horse mackerel *hiraki* — "dressed green fish" or "green fish from the knife;" that is, split, gills and roe removed, gutted, ready for washing and salting.
- Sliced raw cuttlefish and squid, ready to eat.
- Fish balls.
- Shrimp balls.
- Sardines *namaboshi* style — salted, half-dried or soft-cured, with over 40% (and perhaps up to 65%) moisture after drying.
- Dab or flounder.
- Herring roe dipped into seawater, washed, drained, and salted in brine or dry salt.
- Trout.
- Yellow sea bream.
- Mackerel.
- Cockles.
- Eels.
- Sea urchins.
- *Shirasu* — mixture of young herring, sprat and various other small fish.
- Cod roe.
- Pacific barracuda — the Pacific barracuda is reportedly safer to eat at this time than the Atlantic barracuda, according to a Florida specialist in poisoning (ciguetera) caused by fish.
- *Tatami-iwashi* — sardine or anchovy larvae dried on a frame giving the appearance of a thin sheet of paper.
- *Urume-iwashi* — round herring.
- Raw squid slices, ready to eat.
- Boned *fugu* (puffer, globefish) — in Japan, specially trained *fugu*-chefs are licensed to prepare this excellent fish for the table — safely; serious poisoning and fatalities occur when amateurs improperly prepare the puffer.
- Saury.
- Scallops.
- Sablefish (black, blue or coal cod).
- Eel *kabayaki* (see description of *kabayaki* style under canned items).
- Cobia (cabio, black bonito).
- *Hampen* (also spelled *hanpen*) — shark dumplings made by mixing kneaded shark meat and pounded yam into balls,

then dropping them into boiling water; light and spongy, they float in the soup.

- *Naruto wakame* — *Undaria* species of brown seaweed dried by sprinkling with ashes, and then washed and re-dried.

Instant sea products distributed by Japan Food Corporation include:

- Pulverized agar agar gelatin.
- Shrimp curry.

Japan Food Corporation's refrigerated marine products include:

- Cuttlefish *shiokara* — fermented and salted viscera and slices of meat.
- Skipjack (ocean bonito) *shiokara.*
- Sea urchin *shiokara.*
- Crab mix.
- Red (salmon) roe.
- Lumpfish roe.
- Herring roe and brown seaweed.
- Fish sausage.

Seaweed and other sea products distributed by Japan Food Corporation include:

- *Tarako furikake* — salt-cured roe seasoning compound.
- *Kaiso* salad — assorted red, brown and green seaweeds.
- *Kanten* — agar agar gelatin.
- *Kombu* (also spelled *konbu*) — brown seaweed, kelp, sea cabbage, or tangle of *Laminaria* species.
- *Nori* — red laver of *Porphyra* species.
- *Wakame* — brown seaweed of *Undaria* species.

Another importer and distributor of Far Eastern marine products, *Central Boeki (USA), Ltd.,* imports the sea products listed below. Each item is followed by the importer's comments on the product:

- *Dashi kombu* — seaweed for making soup stock.
- *Hayani kombu* — seaweed for cooking with soy sauce and seasoning.
- *Shio kombu* — seaweed preserved with salt and soy sauce, to be eaten as is with rice.
- *Nori* — paper-thin blackish seaweed (of red laver kind).
- *Wakame* — tender seaweed for salad, bean soup, clear soup.

- *Kuki wakame* — stem *wakame* for salads.
- *Tororo kombu* — dried tangle, shredded finely after dipping in vinegar; for clear soup.
- *Oboro* — finer than *tororo kombu;* also used for clear soup.
- *Ne kombu* — bottom stem of *kombu* seaweed used for salads.
- *Hijiki* — seaweed to be cooked with vegetables and seasoned with soy sauce and sugar.
- *Ao noriko* — powdered *nori* used for flavoring foods.
- *Kanten* — agar agar for making gelatin.
- *Kombu ame* — seaweed candy.
- *Uni* — sea urchin roe for eating raw with sauce and *wasabi* mustard.

The preceding Central Boeki products are available at the following stores:

- Katgiri and Company, Inc.; 224 E. 59 Street; New York, N.Y. 10022. (Mail orders accepted.)
- Mikado; 4709 Wisconsin Avenue, N.W.; Washington, D.C. 20016. (Mail orders accepted.)
- Yates Brothers; 4610 Haines Road; St. Petersburg, Florida 33714.
- Seasia; 651 South Industrial Way; Seattle, Washington 98124.

The *Miyako Mutual Trading Company* (431 Crocker Street, Los Angeles, California 90031) supplies the following sea vegetables.

- *Hijiki* — seaweed for cooking with other vegetables and soy sauce.
- *Musubi nori* — dried laver.
- *Ne konbu* (or *kombu*) — kelp root.
- *Oboro konbu* — shredded *konbu.*
- *Tororo konbu* — shaved *konbu.*
- *Ito wakame* — string *wakame* (brown seaweed).
- *Izumo wakame* — flat *wakame.*
- *Naruto wakame* — dried *wakame.*
- *Nama wakame* — salted fresh *wakame.*
- *Shiro kanten* — white agar.
- *Aka kanten* — red agar.

And the following fish:

- *Hanakatsuo* — dried bonito shavings.

- *Kensaki surume* — dried cuttlefish.
- *Tazukuri* — dried sardines.
- *Sake kasuzuke* — frozen salmon and rice.
- Frozen *Hiraki* — split or "half-dried" fish ready for salting.
- Plus abalone, cockles, fish roe of various kinds, etc.

A FINAL LOOK AT THE SEA

In a one-man liferaft during a North Atlantic storm

Bring me to the edge of the sea
Whence I came long before I became me.
Set me adrift upon the swelling tide
And let me sail over to life's other side.
Let me ride high upon the billowing bosom far above the deep deep...
...before winging down into sleep sleep...

H. H. Hirschhorn

Index

A

Abalone, 57, 87, 95, 199, 201
Acid stomach, 131-132 *(see also* indigestion and gastrointestinal distress)
Agar, 141, 203
Alaska pollack, 40
  roe, 80
Albacore tuna, 38, 56
  back skin, 43
Alewife, 60
  roe, 80
Alfonsino, 40
Algae, freshwater, 125-126
  marine *(see* seaweed)
Allergic conditions, 161, 165
Allspice, 112
Almond milk, 153-154
Aloe, 171-172
Ambergris, 139-140
American butterfish, 61
  shad, 55, 73
Amino acids, 21, 28-29, 128
Anchovies, 60, 77, 108, 113, 202
Anemia, 82, 135, 151, 191
Anglerfish, 60
Antacid, 131-133
Arkshells, 199, 201
Arthritis *(see* joint pain)
Asthma, 134, 147, 153, 161, 164, 188, 192
Atherosclerosis, 21, 150

B

Barnacles, 51, 97-98
Barracuda, 61, 118, 202
Bass, 40, 55, 117
Bath additives:
  bed, how to give, 185-186
  cold, 183-184

Bath additives: *(cont.)*
  herbal, 189-193
  how to use, 189-193, 197
  hot water, 183-185
  hot sand, 54
  seawater, 54, 164
  seawater, artificial, 182-183
  sauna, 185
  sitz, 187
  spray or stream with bidet, 187
  spray or stream with hose, 187
  sun, 173-175
  warm, 183-184
Bikini dermatitis, 169-170
Blenny, 40
Blood:
  clots, 149
  high pressure, 150-151, 183, 186
  low pressure, 191
  stopping of, 46-47, 149, 159
Blue rayfish, 41
Bluefish, 55, 61
Bluefin tuna, 38, 40-41
Bone ash, 45-46
  infections, 192-193
Bonito, 61, 201
Bream, 38
Breast cancer, 184
Bromine, 165
Bronchial asthma, 161, 165
Bronchitis, 150, 152-153, 186, 188
Bruises, 24, 193
Burns, 151, 171, 187

C

Caffeine, 163
Calcium, 21, 49, 94, 118, 127, 165
Calories, 37, 54-58
Cardamon, 119
Carbohydrates, 36-37, 94, 128
Carp, 38, 41, 55, 62, 77
  how to pickle, 116-117
  roe, 80, 82

Catfish, 44, 62
  how to pickle, 116-117
  how to prepare, 62-63
Cattails, 161-162
Caviar *(see* roe)
Cayenne pepper, 54, 148-149
Cholesterol, 21, 35-36, 135
Chub mackerel, 40, 42
Cinnamon, 120
Circulation, 164-165, 185-186
Clams, 21, 36, 41-42, 57-58, 77, 89-90,
  105, 117, 199
Clam shell, 51
Cloves, 120
Cobalt, 44
Cobia, 202
Cockles, 91, 202
Cod, 40, 42, 47, 55, 63, 77, 109, 201
  how to prepare, 64
  red, 38
  roe, 80
  salt, how to wash out, 48-49
Colds, flu-like infections and respi-
    ratory tract conditions, 135,
    138, 146-147, 152, 154, 158,
    161, 171, 185-186, 188, 191
Conch, 87-88
Constipation, 120, 136, 141, 151,
    154, 166, 172
Copper, 37, 44, 94
Coral, 51, 133 *(see also* roe)
Corns, 146
Corvina, 117, 148
Cough and throat irritations, 150,
    152-153
Court-bouillon, how to make, 109
Crabs, 57, 101, 105, 109, 199, 203
  blue, 51, 57
  horseshoe, 51
Crawfish, 57, 98, 132
Crayfish, 57, 98
Croaker or drum 136

Curative plants, 25, 200
  herbal baths, 191-193
  how to brew, 197
  how to preserve, 196
  spices, 119-120
  when to collect, 195-196
Currents, 166
Cusk, 64
Cuttlefish, 86-87, 199-203, 205

D

Dead Sea and Sea of Galilee, 160-
    161, 165, 169
Diabetes, 36, 82, 161, 164, 172, 184,
    192
Dilation of body orifices, 142
Dogfish, 40, 64

E

Ear ache or ear conditions, 151, 188
Eczema, 160, 163
Edema, 146, 150
Eel, 34, 41-42, 65-66, 111, 199, 202
  conger, 40, 108
  freshwater, 40
  how to prepare, 65
Eelgrass fertilizer, 51
Eye inflammation, 187-188
  cinder in, 136
  wash, 23, 192

F

Fainting, 24
Fats, oils, lipids, 33-34, 37, 94 *(see
    also* cholesterol and fat per-
    centage under individual fish

Fats, oils, lipids: *(cont.)*
    names in Chapter 4)
Fatty acids, unsaturated, 21
Fertilizers from the sea, 50-51
Festered fingers, 24
Fish biscuits, 29
    bones, 21, 49
    brain, 21
    earstones, 131-132
    eyes, 39, 41, 104
    as fertilizer, 51
    flour baby formula, 30
    freshwater, how to use safely,
        105, 110
    gills, 44, 104
    head, 40
    heart, 42
    high-fat & low protein, 77
    intestines, 77
    kidney, 41
    liver, 21, 36, 40-41 *(see also* oil)
    low-fat & high protein, 77
    low-fat & low protein, 77
    low-fat & very-high protein, 77
    meat, dark, 39, 41, 108
    meat, white, 42
    medium-fat & high protein, 77
    protein supplement, 30
    safe signs for food fish, 103
    sauce, fermented, 113-114
    sauce, natural, 68 *(see also* Chap-
        ters 4, 6 and 7 under indi-
        vidual fish, mollusc or
        crustacean)
    skin, 40-43, 47
    slime, test for skate freshness, 104
    spinal cord, 75
    soup, how to make, 111
    spleen, 42
    stomach, 77, 136
    swim-bladder, 136
Fits and convulsions, 24

Flounders, 66, 77, 202 (dab)
Fluorine, 21, 44, 47
Folic acid, 42
Foot problems, 188, 191-193

G

Gallstones, 154, 160
Garlic, 149-151
Ginger, 120
Goby, 42, 108
Gout, 126, 147, 166, 186, 191-192
Grouper, 40
Gum disease, 150

H

Hair remover, 137
    growth, 139, 140, 154
    and scalp conditions, 191
Halibut, 39-40, 55, 66, 77, 109
Haddock, 34, 41, 55, 66, 77, 109
    roe, 80
Hake, 77, 109
Harvest fish, 40
Headache, 186-187
    menopausal, 24, 146
    migraine, 188
    nervous, 163
Head cold, 21
Heart, 154, 163-165, 183, 186, 188
Heartburn, 23 *(see also* indigestion
    and gastrointestinal distress)
Hemorrhoids, 150, 154, 185, 187-
    189, 192-193
Herring, 31, 39, 41-42, 55-56, 67, 77,
    83, 110-111, 114-117, 201-202
    how to cure before pickling, 114-
        116
    roe, 80, 82, 202-203

Hoarseness, 152
Hogfish, 40

I

Ichthyosis (or scaly-skin disease),
    163
Indigestion and gastrointestinal dis-
    tress, 23, 46, 82, 119, 136, 141,
    147-148, 150-151, 183, 186,188,
    191-192 *(see also* constipation)
Insomnia, 185-186
Insulin, 37, 73, 161
Iodine, 21, 44, 47, 49, 54, 123, 127,
    141, 158-159, 165
Iron, 21, 37, 94
Irritated eyes, 23
Itch, 146 *(see also* skin conditions)
Itching hives, 24

J

Jack mackerel, 42
Joint pain, 24, 134, 182, 186

K

Kelp *(see* seaweed)
Kidney gravel and stones, 151, 166,
    186
Kingfish, 117

L

Lamprey, 38, 40-43
    how to prepare, 43
Lanternfish, 40
Lecithin, 82, 135
Lemon, 108-109, 145-148

Limes, 148
Limpet, 88
Liver and spleen problems, 148, 150,
    191
Liver, Atlantic mackerel, 42
    bluefin tuna, 42
    herring, 42
    seal, 40
    whale, 40
    yellowfin tuna, 42
Lizardfish, 40
Lobster, 35, 57, 98, 109, 117
    Norway, 99
Lumbago, 185, 188-189
Lumpfish, 203

M

Mackerel, 31, 34, 40-42, 69, 77, 83,
    110, 116-117, 199, 202
    back skin, 43
    milt and roe, 80
    skipjack, 38
Magnesium, 20, 94, 165
Manganese, 94
Marjoram, 120
Marinotherapeutic spas and resorts:
    in Belgium, 177
    in France, 178-179
    in Germany, 176-177
    in Spain, 179-180
    in Yugoslavia, 180
Meagre, 136
Menhaden, 38
Menstrual conditions, 150, 159, 186
Milt *(see* roe)
Minerals, 20, 58, 128, 162 *(see also*
    water, mineral)
    daily minimum, 45
    test for, 45
Mud:
    peat, 169

Mud: *(cont.)*
  sea, 168-169
  sea, radioactive, 168
Mullet, 42, 69, 77
  gray, 42
  roe, 80
Mussels, 58, 92, 105, 117
  how to prepare, 92
  shells, 51
Mustard seed, 120

N

Names of sea animals and plants,
    how to avoid confusion, 25-26
Natural rhythms, 21
Nausea, 146-147
Niacin, 37, 42, 108
Nicotinic acid, 94
Northern pike, 39

O

Obesity, 53-54, 160, 185
Ocean catfish, 62
  perch, 56, 77, 109
Octopus, 58, 85-86, 199, 201
  how to prepare, 86
Oil:
  alligator tongue, 134
  angler, 41
  cod, 41
  halibut, 173
  ling, 41
  olive, 151, 154
  pike, 136
  shark, 73, 110
  turbot, 41
  turtle, 134-135
Olives, 154-155
Onion, 148-149, 151-153

Oyster, 35-37, 41-42, 44, 58, 77, 92-
    95, 199
  how to prepare, 86
  shell, 51
  stew or soup, how to prepare,
    93-94

P

Pain control, 183, 185-189, 192
Parrotfish, 40
Papaya, 148
Pepper, 120
Perch, 39, 56, 77, 109, 136
Periwinkle, 87-89
Phlebitis, 186
Phosphorus, 21, 37, 49, 94, 118
Pike, 55, 109
Pike-perch, 38-39
Pilchard, 69
Pityriasis, 163
Plaice, 131
Plankton, 124
Pollack, 41, 77
  heart, 42
Pollen, 161-162
Pond smelt, 108
Porgy, 40, 108
Portuguese man-of-war, 171
Potassium, 20, 94, 127, 165
Prawn, 99
  deep-water, 100
Premature birth, 159
Prostatitis, 161
Protein, 21, 27-28, 31-32, 37, 94, 128
    (see also protein percentages
    under individual fish names in
    Chapter 4)
Pruritis, 163
Psoriasis, 160, 163
Puffer, 202
Pyoderma, 163

Q

Queenfish, 136

R

R-month, 94
Rays, 74
Red drum, 70
  snapper, 44
  steenbras, 40
Redfish, 38, 70
Rheumatism, 120, 134, 140, 147, 150, 154, 159, 166, 168, 172, 185, 189, 191-192
Riboflavin *(see* vitamin B $_2$)
Roach, 38
Rockfish, 40-41, 77, 111
Roe and caviar, 21, 41, 55, 79-83
  how to prepare, 83

S

Sablefish, 70, 202
Sailfish, 71
Saithe, 70
  roe, 80
Salmon, 31, 34, 40, 45, 56, 71-72, 77, 109, 110, 201, 205
  bones, 21
  roe (red caviar), 55, 80, 203
Salt, 21-24, 165-166
  how to get rid of it, 47-49
Sand, 168
Sardines, 31-34, 36, 38, 41-42, 56, 72, 77, 108, 110, 199-200, 202, 205
Sauces *(see* fish sauce)
Saury, 41, 73, 199-202
Scallop, 58, 77, 91, 202
  roe, 81
Sciatica, 188-189, 192

Scorpionfish, 111
Sea anemone, 51, 136-137
  beef, 21
  bream, 61
  cabbage, 128, 203
  cucumber, 51, 200
  egg, 82
  foods, Far Eastern, available in the USA, 199-205
  foods, how to barbecue, 108
  foods, how to broil, 108
  foods, how to can, 118-119
  foods, how to conserve vitamins, 108
  foods, how to debone, 108
  foods, how to hold together while cooking, 108
  foods, how to pickle, 114-118
  foods, how to poach, 83, 108
  foods (freshwater), how to safely keep freshly caught ones, 105
  lettuce, 126
  mud, 51, 168-169
  snakes, 140
  stings, 171
  turtle, 121-122
  urchin, 137-138, 203
  urchin roe, 81
Seabather's eruption, 170-171
Seacoast climate and atmosphere, 54, 157-159
Seawater drinking, 22, 164-166
  how to collect, 181-182
Seaweed, 50-51, 54, 123-129, 141-143, 162, 199, 203
  how to select and prepare, 125
Sexual exhaustion, 73, 82, 98, 150
Shark, 39, 73-74, 108, 199
  dumplings, 202
  flour, 29
  how to cook, 73-74
  soupfin, 40
Shellfish, how to steam-cook, 101-102

Shrimp, 31, 34-35, 51, 57, 77, 100, 117, 200-203
  how to pickle, 100
Siscowet lake trout, 77
Silver perch, 136
Skates and rays, how to cook, 74
Skin conditions and health, 134, 147, 151, 153-154, 163, 186, 189, 191-193
Skipjack, 41-43, 74, 77, 203
Snail operculum, 132-133
Sodium, 19, 22, 47, 94, 165 *(see also* salt)
Sole, 74
Sore throat, 23, 147, 152-153, 166, 186
Spider, scorpion, insect, etc. bites and stings, 139, 172
Sponge, 51, 138
Sprains, 24, 192-193
Sprat or brisling, 34, 74
Squid, 58, 86-87, 199-200, 202
Starfish, 51, 139
Sterility, 159
Stomach function and problems *(see* indigestion and gastrointestinal distress)
Stones, 191-192 *(see also* kidney gravel and stones, and urinary tract)
Sturgeon, 55, 75
Sun, 163-164, 172
  lotions and ointments, 134, 147, 172-174
Sunlight, 163
Swimmer's itch, 171
Swordfish, 38, 40, 56, 76

T

Tan, how to safely, 174-175
Thermal packs and compresses, 186-189
Thiamine *(see* vitamin B $_1$)

Tides, 166
Tone, 154, 184-185
Tonic, 24, 135
Toothache, 23, 150
Trace elements, 44, 182 *(see also* individual chemical elements)
Trout, 42, 56, 76-77, 202
Tuberculosis, 159
Tuna, 31, 34, 38-41, 56, 76, 111, 117, 201
Turbot, 55, 109
Turtle bouillon, how to prepare, 121

U

Urinary tract problems and health, 143, 150-151, 163, 167, 185-187, 192 *(see also* stones)

V

Vanadium, 36
Varicose veins, 188-189
Vinegar, 108, 114, 140, 150, 166
Vitamin A, 21, 37, 39-40, 43, 110, 112, 126, 135, 161, 191
  B, 108, 126. 191
  B $_1$, 37, 40, 82, 94, 127
  B $_2$, 37, 42, 82, 94
  B $_6$, 41
  B $_{12}$, 21, 41
  C, 41, 49, 123, 126-128, 145
  D, 21, 38-39, 110, 135, 191
  E, 41, 191
  H, 135
  K, 135
Vitamins, 162
  water-soluble, how to save, 38
Viziga (spinal cord delicacy), 75
Vomiting of blood, 23

W

Walleye pollock, 77
Water, drinking, 54, 160, 166, 188
    mineral, 166-167
Watercress, 49 *(see also* curative
    plants)
Weakfish, 117, 136
Wet grass treatment, 184
White fish vs. fatty fish, 111
Whale, 21, 40
Whelk, 89
Whitefish, 37

Whiting, 77
Worms, 150, 154
Wound healing, 163, 189, 192-193

Y

Yellow sea bream, 202
Yellowfin tuna, 38, 40-41

Z

Zinc, 37, 44